AUGUSTA COUNTY, VIRGINIA

SURVEY BOOK
OF
JAMES PATTON AND WILLIAM PRESTON

1752–1755

James L. Douthat

Heritage Books
2024

HERITAGE BOOKS

AN IMPRINT OF HERITAGE BOOKS, INC.

Books, CDs, and more—Worldwide

For our listing of thousands of titles see our website
at
www.HeritageBooks.com

A Facsimile Reprint
Published 2024 by
HERITAGE BOOKS, INC.
Publishing Division
5810 Ruatan Street
Berwyn Heights, MD 20740

Originally published 2009
Mountain Press
Signal Mountain, Tennessee

International Standard Book Number
Paperbound: 978-0-7884-2773-2

JAMES PATTON

Survey Book also used by William Preston
1752 - 1755

Once in a great while one finds a very unique collection of material that will give some new insight into the times of our ancestors. This little book was just such a find. It is a hand stitched little leather book that had at one time gotten wet and some fading occurred from that and at some other time either rats or insects destroyed one corner of the material. The parts that could be read were very interesting.

This is more or less an abstraction of the material as we have left out some of the surveyor's calls which give directions and distances of each line of the survey. You can read most of these in the material. We chose to leave them out as they are meaningless for the most part as you would never find the original tree or pile of rocks on the river bank or just what point on the side of the hill. These points are necessary for the exact location of the tract in question. We have included the names of persons, creeks/rivers and mountains or meadows when given that will put you in the neighborhood of the property.

The Survey Book for Augusta County is one of the earliest of their land records. Probably you can go to their court records and find the deed filed there in the name of the person for whom this was the survey. James Patton was one of the earliest surveyors for the western portion of the state and he is followed by his nephew William Preston. At one point in the book, the whole book was turned over and the records start in the back of the book and come forward. At some point in the life of the book, someone who was not the original owner or surveyors, numbered the pages from the front to the back. When the book is turned over and the records come from the back to the front, the original page numbers become all fouled up and do not run in sequence. We have tried to keep them as close to the original direction so the material flows in a logical fashion.

Spelling is one of the interesting portions of the book. There did not seem to be an exact spelling order for a lot of names, especially the "Catawba" River. It is spelled a dozen different ways all by the same person. In reading this you will need to read it as it sounds and use your best judgement as to the correct spelling. We have written it just as it was originally and have made little or no attempt to correct. However, certain words that are used frequently, and we know they are misspelled, we have place a [sic] after that word to indicate "this is how it is written, but we know it is not right".

The original of this piece can be found in the Wytheville Community College Library in the Kegley Collection. They also do have a photocopy of the materials from which the copies are made for this book. In reading it, I did got to the original for some corrections and you may not be able to read all of a page, but the original is somewhat easier to read. When something is totally missing, there is no way we will guess what is said or meant, we just leave it blank.

Enjoy the material and I hope that you can find some of your ancestors here.

James L. Douthat
Signal Mountain, Tennessee
2009

****

No 84

James Pattons

[illegible]

Augusta

****

[illegible] Place on Meadow Creek [illegible]
[illegible] 40 E 238 [illegible] line S25 E 140 [illegible]
S75 E [illegible] Acres [illegible]

Thos Brroneger Dr to JP
To 66 Acres of land — 7 [illegible]
3 years Interest — 1 2 6
2 Pts 12/6 Pat Fee 10/6 — 1 3 [illegible]
Surveyors Fee — 1 11 3
11 6 [illegible]

John Highley 63 acres — [illegible]
2 Pts 12/6 Pat Fee 10/6 — 1 3 [illegible]
Sur Fee — 1 11 [illegible]
[illegible]

John Brroneger 100 Acres — 10
2 years Interest — 1 15 [illegible]
2 Pts 12/6 Pat Fee 10/6 Sur Fee 31/3 — 2 15 [illegible]
11 [illegible]

2

Page 2 Mr. Vauss' place in Meadow Creek - house Willson's land.

****

Tho's Barineger do to J.P.

To 66 acres of land	£7	10	0
years interest	1	2	6
2 Rts 12/6 Pat Fee 10/6	1	3	0
Surveyors Fee	1	11	3
	11	6	9

****

John Kighler** 63 acres	£7	10	0
2 Rts 12/6 Pat Fee 0/6	1	0	0
Sur'ys Fee	1	11	0
	£10	4	0

****

John Brineger 100 acres	£7	10	0
2 years interest	0	1	0
2 Rts 12/6 Pat Fee 10/6			
Frs. Fee 31/3	2	13	0
	11	3	0

** Could be read "Highler"

Jacob hermon Dr

to 1110 acers of Lande where he now Lives at 100 acers for £30 as per agreement	31	10	0
to 23 Rights at 5/ 3d Each	7	3	9
Survairs & Patent fees	2	1	9
Cash Lent you	0	6	9
	£41	1	

Captn adam hermon Dr

To 543 acers where he now Lives at 100 for £30	14	17	4
to Survairs & Patent fees	2	1	9
to 11 rights at 5/ 3d Each	3	5	9
	£20	7	

14
1 9
16

3

****

Page 3 Jacob Hermon

50 1110 acres of Lande where he now lives at 1100 acres for £30 as per agreement to 23 Rights - - - each

	£7	3	9
Suveyors & Patent fees	2	1	9
Capt. Les Ayou	0	6	9

Note: on page 4 - by your bond this 26 of March 1751/2 payable first of May inset.

	£41	1	9

****

Capt'n Adam Hermon do

5143 acres where he now lives at 1100 for £30

	14	17	4
to surveyors & patent fee	2	1	9
to 11 rights at 5/ per each	3	8	9

Note: on page 4 - by your bond this first of April

	11	0	0
1754 payable in May inset	11	15	0
by cash	8	12	10
	£20	7	10

John Miller Dr to J P — Dr

	£	s	d
to 125 acres Land survayed by Mr Poge	6	5	0
to 60 acres survayed by Mr Buchanan	3	0	0
to 2 survayors fees & 2 patent fees	4	3	6
to 5 Rights at 5 s Ster Each is	1	11	3
	£14	19	

James Harris of Cripple Creek Dr

	£	s	d
to 2050 acres Land at £4 : 5 per	87	2	6

1754 James McColl to J P Dr

	£	s	d
to 100 acres where he now Lives	5	0	0
to 520 acres neigh Wm Calhouns Land	26	0	0
to 2 survayors fees & 2 patent fees	4	3	6
to 13 Rights at 5 s Ster Each	3	18	3
	£39	2	

5

Page 5 John Miller due fee to J.P.

50 125 acres of land surveyed by Mr. Page

	£	s	d
	£ 6	5	0
to 60 acres surveyed by Mr. Buckanan	3	0	0
to 2 surveyors fee & 2 patent fee	4	3	6
to 5 rights at 5/ per each is	1	11	3
	£14	19	9

Note: on page 6 - by your Bond this April 1754

	£	s	d
	£11	0	0
by cash	3	14	4
	£14	14	4

****

James Harris of Criple [sic] Creek - do

to 2050 acres of land at £4/50 per

£87 2 6

Note: on Page 6 - by your Bond of April 1754 payable the night of April 1753 with interest from April 1754 for by an abetment of £87 0 0

	£	s	d
		2	6
	£87	2	6

****

James McCall to J.P.

	£	s	d
To 100 acres where he now lives	£80	0	0
to 520 acres neigh Wm. Calhonas land	26	0	0
to 2 surveyors fee & 2 patent fee	4	3	6
to 13 Rights at 5/ per each	3	18	3
	£34	2	9

Note: on Page 6 - by your bond of the 9 April 1754 - payable in April 1759 with interest £34 0 0

	£	s	d
by abetment given surveyor of		2	-
	£34	2	-

****

Sir James Miller to JP — Dr

to 700 acers of Land where he now Lives	35	0	0
to survairs & patent fees	2	1	9
to 14 Rights at 5/7 Each	4	6	4
	41	8	1

Robert Novis to JP — Dr

to 180 acers where he Lives at £4-5-0	7	13	0
to A survairs fee on Do	1	11	
	£9	4	

Jo Miller
James, widow Lives & sons to JP — Dr

to 400 acers of Land at £4-5-0 per 100	17	0	0
to A survairs fee & patent fee	2	1	9
to 1050 acers at £5 per	52	10	0
	71	11	[illegible]

7

Page 7 James Willey to J.P. do

to 700 acres of land where he now lives			
	£35	0	0
to surveyors & patent fee	2	1	9
to 14 Rights at 5/ per each	4	6	4
	£41	8	1

Note: on Page 8 - by his Bond of 18 of April 1759 - payed the 12 April inset with interest for:

	£39	3	0
by an abetment made him of			
	2	5	1
	£41	8	1

****

Robert Noris to J.P. Do

to 180 acres where he lives at			
£ 4 5 0	£7	13	0
to surveyors fee and do	1	11	-
	£8	4	-

Note: on Page 8 by cash 14 April 1757

	£9	4	5

****

James Miller & widow lives & sons to J.P. Do

to 400 acres of land at 55 per 100			
	£17	0	0
to a surveyors fee & patent fee			
	2	1	3
to 1040 acres at £5 per	52	10	0
	£71	11	3

Note: on Page 8 - by bonde payable in April 1753

	£64	10	-
by 100 acres not in the survey			
	5	0	-
by ye surveyors fee & patent fee			
	2	0	-
	£71	10	-

****

****

John & Robert Mc farland Dr

	£	s	d
1020 to 1020 where Robert Lives att £5 per 100	51		
John Mc farland to J Walk[?] Dr			
to 361 acers 327 & 106 acers 793 at £5 per	39	13	0
survoirs fees & 3 patent fees	5	14	9
to Rights at 5 s Each	5	6	8
	51	14	6
	50	15	3

Robert Mc farland Dr

	£	s	d
248 acers where downey Lives at £5	12	8	0
Rights survoirs & patent fees	3	13	0
	16	1	0

Ezekel Collhoun Dr

	£	s	d
500 acers where he Lives 100 for £30	13	15	6
10 rights survoirs & patent fees	5	4	2
	18	14	3

Patrick Colhoun Dr

	£	s	d
to 159 acers at £4 : 5 . 0 per 100	6	14	7
3 rights survoirs & patent fees	3	1	6
	9	15	1

9

****

Page 9 John & Robert McFarland do
for 1020 where Robert lives at £5 per 100

	£54	0	0
by their bond this 12 April 1754			
	£54	0	0

John McFarland to J.P. do
367 acre 327 & 106 acres 798 at £5 per

	£39	13	0
surveyors fee & 3 patent fees			
	£ 5	14	3
7 Rights at 5£ per each	5	8	8
	£54	14	3
	£50	15	3
by your bond 20 April 1754 for			
	£24	18	-
by £9 4 9 pd Col. M. Buchanan			
	9	4	9
by Cash this 20 April 1754	16	11	-
	£50	14	3

Robert McFarland do per contra

248 acres where Downey lives at £5

	£12	8	0
Rights, surveys and patent fees	3	13	0
	£16	1	0
by bond this 12 April 1754	£ 7	9	5
by cash to Mr. Buchanon	8	13	7
	£16	1	12

****

Zekel Callhoun do per contra

500 acres where he lives 1100 for £30

	£13	15	6
10 rights, surveys & patent fee	5	4	3
	£18	19	9
by cash this 18 April 1754	£18	19	-

****

Patrick Calhoun do per contra

to 159 acres at £4 5 0 per 100

	£6	14	7
to 3 rights, surveys & patent fees	3	1	0
	£9	15	7
by your bond this 20 of April	£5	16	-
by cash	3	18	-
	£9	15	-

****

****

Alexander Sayers ——	Dr		
To 536 acres on Reeds run at £5 per	26	16	0
To surveyors & Patent fees ——	2	1	9
11 rights att 5/ per Each	3	8	9
	£32	6	6
To 504 acres where he Lives att £4:5:0 —	21	2	0
To surveyors & patent fees ——	2	1	9
To interest on [illegible] two years is £2:6:3	£55	10	3
To one pr milstons & Groves —— 10.0.0	12	13	3
To Cash Lent —— 0.7.6	£68	3	6
Lodwick Stearn senior to J P —	Dr		
To 100 acres run out by mr Poge 1751	7	10	0
To 100 Entered with mr Buchanan in 1744 —	3	0	0
To 200 more in your tract at £5 per —	20	0	0
To 2 surveyors & 2 patent fees per	4	2	6
To 10 kings Rights at 5/ Each	£3	2	6
To interest on Do since april 1749	£37	15	0
John Mountgomery	Dr		
To 646 acres of Land where he Lives	27	9	10
interest on do 2 years & 2 months ——	2	14	6
	30	4	4
To one surveyors fee ——	1	11	[illegible]
	£32	[illegible]	[illegible]

****

Page 11

Alexander Seeyars	do		
to 936 acres on tracts was at £5 per			
	£26	16	0
surveys & patent fees	2	1	9
— rights at 5£ per each	3	8	4
	£32	6	6
to 504 acres where he lives at £4-5-0			
	£21	2	0
to surveys & patent fees	2	1	4
	£55	10	3
to interest on - - - - - years is	£2:6:3		
to one for milstone & groers [?]	£10:0:0		
to cash lent	£0:7:0		
	£68	3	6
by his bond this 22 April 1754	£55	10	-
by his note of this date	12	13	6
	£68	3	6

****

Fredrick Heavn Lewis to J.P.	do	per contra	
to 100 acres was out by Mr. Page 1754			
	£ 7	10	0
to 100 entered with Mr. Buchanon in 1744			
	3	0	0
to 400 more in your tract at £5 per	20	0	0
to 2 surveys & 2 patent fees	4	2	6
to 10 kings Rights at 5£ each	13	2	6
to interest and since 1 April 1749	£37	15	0

M't to enter for Phato Barbee 206 between the Holston land on Craigs Creek.

200 acres for Lewis Getty on west side Lees under y'e mountain
10th Nov'r 1754.

****

John Montgomery	do		
to 646 acres of land where he lives	£27	9	16
to interest on do 2 years & 2 months	2	14	6
	30	4	4
to one surveyors fee	1	11	3
	£32	0	3

****

James Patton to the Company Dr

3810 acres where Dyong Sages lived
400 where Nicelesherfford Entred with Colol woods
4.400 Cold fannet under nockolow mountain
4.000 Springfield bought of Charls harte
2.600 Kill Mc Evenan farmed lay at
Cultivating stock & building
11:750 at 100 for £30 is — 320 11 0

1 sthom saturday 7th of aprill Lodged at John Lyle
2 nyghts at Kinchs one at Millers one then to
Mr Armstrongs the 11th being Friday

13

Page 13

James Patton to the Company do

to 350 acres where Leyon & Seegs lived
to 400 where Wiseley transfered entered with Colon'l Woods
to 4,400 Col'd Sernnet** under Nockalow Mountain
4,000 Springfield bought of Charles Hawts
2,600 - - - - -
cultivating flock & building

11:750 at 1100 for £30 is £320 11 0

Left home Saturday 7th of April lodged at John Lyles 2 nights, at Rennicks one, at Millers one, then to Mr. Armstrongs the 11th back Wednesday.

** Could be "F" or "S" on this word.

Line 2d westcot & widow ewik — £

	£	s	d
To 1047 acers of Land att £5 pr 100	54	17	0
2 years intrest on do from 1 aprail 1749			

Matthew wilkshire — Dr

	£	s	d
to 680 acers at £5 pr 100	34	0	0
to surveirs & patent fees	2	1	9
to 19 rights of 5s / ster each	4	7	6
intrest on do from 1 aprail 1749 £	40	9	3
	82		

[illegible]b Coffel — Dr

	£	s	d
60 acers where he Lives	9	0	0
survirs & patent fees	2	1	9
4 Rights at 5s / ster each	1	5	0
intrest on do from 1 aprail 1749	12	6	9

15

****

Page 15

- - binet'r Westcot & widow Elswick

to 1097 acres of land at £5 per 100

	£54	17	0
2 years interest on do from 1 April 1749.			

****

Natheniel Willas heir do per contra

to 640 acres at £5 per 100	£34	0	0
to surveyor & patent fees	2	1	4
to 14 rights at 5s per each	4	7	6
interest on do from 1 April 1749	£40	9	3

****

Jacob Caslel do per contra

80 acres where he lives	£ 9	0	-
surveyor & patent fees	2	1	9
4 Rights at 5s per each	1	5	0
interest on do from 1 April 1749	£12	6	9

****

Andrew Ewins —

347 acers where he Lives at £ —	17	7
Surveiors & patent fees —	2	1
76 Rights at 5/- —	£2	3
interest on Do from 1 april 1749 —	£21	11

interest on Do from 1 aprin

17

Page 17

Andrew Evans

to 347 acres where he lives at £5	£17	7	-
to surveyor & patent fees	2	1	0
to 7 rights at 5s per	2	3	-
to interest on do from 1 April 1749	£21	11	-

****

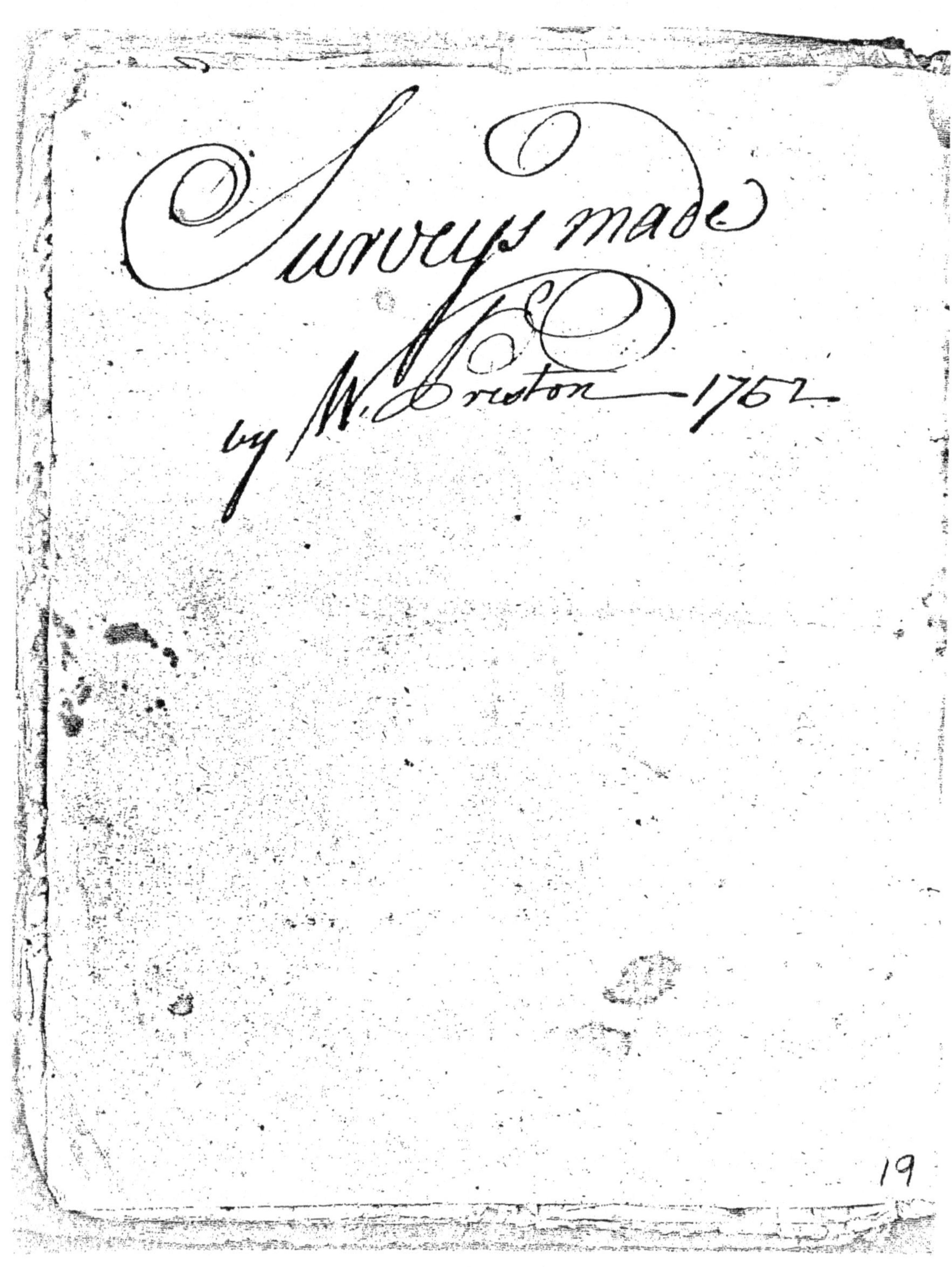
Surveys made
by W. Preston 1752
19

Page 18 - blank

Page 19

SURVEYS MADE BY W. PRESTON 1752

From here on the records are as those of surveys and not the accounting as in the first seventeen pages.

16 Decr. 1752 Wm Hutchison on ye Waters of Catawbo

Beg: at a B, O, in his own line

	Poles	
East	58	to 2 Hicorys on a High Hill — Rec'd
N 8 E	60	to a white Oak
West	50	to a W, O. Saplin in his line thence to ye Beg:
S 19 W	63	

+ Containing 20 Acres

16 Decr. 1752 James Davies on a branch of Catawbo
Beg at 2 B, Od being a corner with Col Buchanan
made Neatte Moores Land at the great road side —

N45 W	60	to 3 R O: Sap: on a Hill —
S 70 W	116	to 2 W, & 1 B O: in a Hollow
S 40 W	18	to a W. & B O on a Hill -
S —	116	to a W, O Sap:
N 55 E	28	to a R, B, & Hicory Saps being an old Corner above the great Road next to Clyd

Col Buchanan has the other Courses which I must get at Reed Creek — — —

20th Decr. 1752 Surveyed for James Bean on ye South Side of Roanoke a tract of Land. Beg: at 3 White Oak Saplins in his Own

+

N 51 E	40 poles	line to 2 white Oak saplins Rec'd
N 23 W	100	to 2 White Oak saplins
S 77 W	120	to a Black Oak in a line of Pattersons Land which is the same course of Beans Line & with the same to the Beginning — — —

95 95 Acres
20—

Page 20

16 Dec. 1752
Wm. Hutchison on ye waters of Catawba - beg. At a B.O. in his own line - containing 20 acres.

16 Dec'r 1752
James Davieson a branch of Catawba - beg. At 2 B.O. - being a corner with Col. Buchanan made neath Moore's land at the great roadside - being an old corner above the great road next to Clyd, Col. Buchanan has the other courses which I must get at Reed Creek.

[Note: The above entry is crossed out.]

20th Dec'r 1752
Surveyed for James Bean on ye south sides of Roanoke tract of land. Beg: at 3 white oak saplins [sic] in his own line - adj. Line of Patterson's land which is the same course of Bean's line & with the same to the Beginning. - 95 acres.

****

22d. Decmbr. 1752		Surveyed for William Bonar a tract of Land on Both sides of Roanoke Begining at a Locust by a Bank on the South side of the River in a line of Thomas Robisons Land & with said Line
N76W	86	to 2 poplars & an Ash in Robinsons Corner opposite to ye falls of Meadow Run —
S62W	60	to a Walnut — — —
S70W	100	to a Locust & Red Oak Saplins on a hill side
South	96	poles 20 to the River & up the same to a Hicory on ye Bank
N59E	270	~~to a ...~~ to the Begining
		Containing 92 Acres Recd
22d. Decr. 1752		Survd. for John McCurry a tract of Land on Both sides of
on ye South side		Roneoke Beg: at a Red Oak & Locust Sapt. corner to Wm Bonr
S52W	60	to a Hicory & Red Oak Sap.
S20W	100	to 3 Hicorys
N72W	40	to 2 Hicory Saplins Recd
S45W	140	to a Pine by a bank
South —	20	Crossing the River to an Ash on ye Bank
S50W	72	up the River
S75E	120	to a pine ~~on a high Bank~~ thence ~~to ye Beg~~
N39E	253	
~~North~~ —	120	to ye Beg crossing ye River 204 Acres
22d. Decr. 1752		Thomas Willson on ye South side of Roanoke Beg: at a Sugr. tree by the Bank of the River called ye South Fork
S22W	80	to a pine on a Hill
S66E	100	to a Hicory Recd
N60E	40	to the River thence Down the same to the Beg
		containing 41 Acres

21

Page 21

22'd December 1752 - Surveyed for William Bonar a tract of land on both sides of Roanoke. Beginning at a locust by a bank on the south side of the River in a line of Thomas Robisons land & with said line. At a corner of Robinson's opposite to ye falls of Meadow Run - 92 acres.

22'd Dec'r 1752 - Sur'd for John McCurry a tract of land on both sides of on ye south side Roanoke. Beg: at a red oak & locust sap'l corner to Wm. Bonar - 204 acres.

22'd Dec'r 1752 - Thomas Willson on ye south side of Roanoke. Beg: at a sug'r tree by the bank of the River called ye south fork. - 41 acres.

22d Decr 1752		Sur: for Samuel Jackson on both sides of Roanoke Beg: at a Walnut by a bank on the S side & Down the same
N 05 W	48	to a Locust
S 14 E	110	to a White Oak
S 46 W	116	to a W Oak on a Step Bank
S 27 E	80	Crossing the River & up the same to 4 poplars on a Hill
N 46 E	134	~~thence down the River to ye Beg~~
N 10 W	170	Containing 92 acres Recd
22d Decr 1752		Surveyd for Wm McCurry a tract of Land on Both sides of Roanoke Beg: at a Walnut by a Gully on ye South side of the River & up the same & ~~Crossing~~
S 43 W	48	Crossing the River to a Beech on the Bank
S 70 W	106	to 2 Hiccory Sap: at ye foot of a Hill on ye North Fork
S 30 E	80	to 2 red Oaks
~~S 30 E~~	~~20~~	~~to ... in last course~~ Recd
N 75 E	134	to 3 White Oak Saplins thence to ye Beg:
N 16 W	105	~~to ye Beg~~ 80 acres
Sur'd for		Robert Brayson in the Devils Den a Tract
23 Decr 1752		Beg: at a White Oak in a line of John McCurrys Land & With said Line
N 30 E	40	To a pine Crossing the Branch Recd
S 66 E	80	to a Pine
S 20 E	38	to a white Oak
S 55 E	60	to a white Oak on a Hill
S 30 W	45	Crossing the Branch to a Hiccory on a Hillside
N 50 W	175	Down the Branch to the Beg:
		Containing 65 acres

22

Page 22

22'd Dec'r 1752 - Sur'd for Samuel Jackson on both sides of Roanoke. Beg: at a walnut by a bank on the s[outh] side & down the same - 92 acres.

22'd Dec'r 1752 - Survey'd for Wm. McCurry a tract of land on both sides of Roanoke. Beg: at a walnut by a gully on ye south side of the River & up the same & crossing the River to a back on the bank. 80 acres.

23'd Dec'r 1752 - Sur'dy for Robert Brayson in the Devils Den, a tract. Beg. At a white oak in a line of John McCurry's lane & with said line - 65 acres.

29th Decr. 1752 Survd for Adam Lyday a Tract of Land on on both sides of Goose Creek Beg: at a W, O by a Branch on ye S side of the Creek Th:

N 38 W	~~40~~ 38	to a Hiccory in a Line of Patt: Shirkeys Land with his Line
S 43 W	40 —	to his two Corner W Os & with his Line
N 38 W	40	Crossing the Creek to a B O. Sap: th:
S 60 W	186	Down the River to a W, O, on a hill
S 30 E	50	Crossing the Creek to a W, O, at ye mountain foot
N 9 E	~~145~~ 164	~~to ye Beg.~~
N 33 E	90	Beg. 104 Acres Recd

30th Decr. 1752

Surveyed for John Robinson Senr. one Tract of Land on Both sides of Goose Creek Beg: at a white Oak Cor. Corner to another Tract of Land Belonging to Sd Robinson on

S 46 W	60	to 2 W O, Sap th: Recd
S 25 E	160 —	to a W O
N 47 E	72	to a Hiccory at ye foot of a steep Bank at ye Rr
S 40 E	60	Down to where the Bank closes with ye River
N 67 E	45	to a pine Crossing the River
N — —	25	to a Line of Sd Robinsons Land
N 75 W	147	to 2 W Os
N 10 W	106	to ye Beg. 70 acres

23

Page 23

29th Dec'r 1752 - Surv'd for Adam Lyday a tract of land on on [sic] both sides of Goose Creek. Beg: at a W.O. by a branch on ye s[outh] side of the Creek - in a line of Patt. Thirkey's land with his line - 104 acres.

30th Dec'r 1752 - Surveyed for John Robinson, Sen'r one tract of land on both sides of Goose Creek. Beg. At a white oak corner to another tract of land belonging to said Robisson [sic] - 70 acres.

Part of James Davies Survey By Col Buch[anan]

Beging at a Locust on ye E side of sd draft

N40 W	132	2 B O & H[illegible] *
N63 E	38	2 W O to protract
N40 E	40	
N56 E	104	2 B O * to Branch 70
S41 E	120	Large W O to [illegible]

1752	Sur.d	Joshua Hadley a tract of Kings Land on ye
22d D		North Side of James River near ye Hellmoor Bottom
+	Beg	at a W O tree near a Draft thence
		popler by sd Draft
N43 W	46	to protract from ye first popl[ar]
S80 W	120	a poplar & W O
N18 W	40	R O 2 W O
S75 W	42	2 W O Locust
S8 W	40	3 Gum [illegible] Beg
S62 E	160	
N44½ E	100	to ye Beg 95 acres

Record

+	Sur.d	Thomas Brniniger Beg: at a Gum & Poplar on
N45 W	100	to B O & W O corner to Daubnes Land
S25 W	120	2 W O by a Hile (to a run 60)
S68 E	40	3 Pine
S41 E	54	W O on ye [illegible] Side of Bradshaws Creek (to ye Creek 43)
N31 E	100	to ye Beg: 66 acres
20th Feb 1753		

Recd

24

Page 24

22 Dec' 1752 - Sur'd Joshua Hadley a tract of Henry's land on ye north side of James River near ye Halfmoon Bottom. Beg. At a W.O. tree near a draft thence... - 95 acres

- Surv'd for Thomas Briniger Beg.: at a gum & poplar on ye creek - corner to Daubnes land on south side of Bradshaw's Creek - 66 acres.

****

		16th Decr. 1752
		James Davies on a branch of Catawbo Beg at
+		a WO [illegible] thence
N41W	120	2 B O.s (to a branch 50)
N45W	60	3 R O s on a hill
S70W	116	2 WO 1 R O in a hollow Recd.
S40W	18	W.O. B O. on a hill
S---	116	W O s
N55E	28	R O H s
S40E	132	Locust on the E side of a draft
N47½E	179	to ye. Begining 230 acres

Survd. for Wm. Hanley on Cedar Creek		
+ Beginning at a Large B O by a Glade		
S70W	100	to a B O in the naked Land
S33E	40	2 WOs } Protract S48E130 then Protract
S55E	88	
S15E	90.	4 WOs. by a Sink hole
East	40	2 W Os. by a Brook North 166 poles & along
16th Feb.y 1753		the hill 110 poles to ye Begining
		Recd. 120 Acres Exam.

Page 25

16th Dec'r 1752 - James Davies on a branch of Catwaba. Beg. At a W.O. runeth thence - 230 acres.

16th Feb. 1753 - Sur'd for Wm. Hanley on Cedar Creek. Beginning at a large B.O. by a glade...120 acres.

****

21 Feb: 1753 Surd for John Righler on both sides of Bradshaws Creek beg at a Double WO by a bank on ye East side of ye Creek thence crossing

S40E	43	Walnut & RO by a brook (to ye Creek 10)
S37W	160	pines on a Brushy Hill
N55W	84	crossing ye Creek to 4 Ht (to ye Creek 58)

Rec'd

Surd for John Brinizer on bothsides of Bradshaws Creek beg at 4 Ht corner to ye Land of John Righler thence

S38W	102	WO by a steep Bank of the Creek
S66W	120	to a pine in ye Barrens
S41E	80	2 large WOs (to ye Creek 60) on ye E side

Rec'd

Surd for Joseph Camming on ye north fork of Goose Creek beg at 3 WOs on ye South side of the Creek & up the same

N15W	136	crossing ye Creek to 3 pines on a Spur (to ye C: 56)
N70W	56	2 pines by a Lick & a Gum
S40W	100	4 Hs on a Hill (to a brook 56)
----	200	to Protract) S10E235
N80E	32	to a Red O: on ye bank of sd Creek
S10E	[illegible]	crossing & up ye same to a large Rock on ye Bank

175 Acres

Exam'd Plan

Rec'd

26

Page 26

21 Feb. 1753 - Sur'd for John Kighler on both sides of Bradshaw's Creek.

Sur'd fore [sic] John Briniger on both sides of Bradshaw's Creek beg. At 4 H[hickory] & corner to ye land of John Kighler.

Sur'd for Joseph Cummings on ye north fork of Goose Creek - 175 acres.

****

	23d	Feb 7 1753
Surd	for	Erwin Patterson on Tinkers Creek beg:
at a	Hicory	S by a Tilder of Wm [illegible] ham his corner South his Line
S6W	116	H Js by a meadow
S65E	180	3 WOs in a Hollow 3 BOs by a sink hole
~~S6W~~	~~266~~	S33E 132 2 WO
~~S70E~~	~~40~~	S80E 42 2 WOs in ye North line
North	146	WO BOs on a Hill
S70W	66	2 BOs on ye point of a Hill
N21W	110	to a tall BO on ye top of a Hill thence a straight course to ye Beg: which Mr. Mills & Patterson says will not enterfere with the Stone house Pat Land.
	+	
Surd	for	Wm Graham Join ing his own Land beg at
	+	3 WOs in a Hollow
S6W	266	WO BO Pat corner } to Protract
S70E	40 -	
E - - -	36	H & WO under a Mountain
N45E	112	RO & BH by a Gully
N - - -	74	to a WOs corner to Pattersons Land
N80W	42	2 WO trees
N33W	132	3 BOs
N63W	20	3 WOs in a Hollow ye Beg

27

Page 27

23rd Feb 1753 - Sur'd for Erwin Patterson on Tinker Creek adj. Wm. Byrham [?] - "...which Mr. Mills & Patterson says will not enterfere [sic] with the stone house Pat. Land."

Sur'd for Wm. Graham joining his own land adj. Paterson's [sic] land.

26 Feb	1753	Leonard Houff beg: Oak O on a hill
N35W	166	BOWO in a Valey
S70W	82	BOWO (a Run 65)
N75W	80	WO ~~...~~
S65W	162	ROWOs by a swamp (...6) Ingrams corner
S5W	100	Ches: on a spur
S60W	160	WO in a Hollow nigh a spring
S25E	76	2 Ches: on a ~~Hollow~~ Spur
S39W	40	2 BO: WOs (S side of a Hill
S25E	80	Ws by a spring
S17W	60	2 ROWs
E east	56	crossing y Run to a White oak on y E side
N36E	62	up y Run to a WO
N62E	60	BO on a Bank
S70E	80	Leaning BO
N40E	60	WO on a spur
N8W	56	3 WOs ~~Ingram ...~~
N60E	30	2 WO ... Ches: Oak by a run
S60E	68	Chesnut
N30E	108	Ch: } to prote
S50E	110	Ch: on a Rocky hill
N40E	60	BO N side of a Run (run 40) the ...
N50W	136	3 BOs by a Spring & thence
	132	allong the hills to the beg

Bent Mountain

Rec'd

28

Page 28

26th Feb. 1753 - Leneorard [sic] Houff adj. Ingram's corner near Bent Mountain.

****

3	John	Mills Mill Place 28th Feby. 1753
beg. a	White Pine on a Hill on ye West side of a Branch	
S10E	110	crossing ye River to 3 pines in a grove
N50E	180	Chtt WOs in ye Barren to a Run 80
N30E	60	RO
N35W	66	BO on a Ridge nigh a meadow
1st March 1753		Chesnut Rock on Huffs Creeke beg. a
		3 RO's on a steep Bank
N20W	34	~~Double WOs on a ridge~~ pine by 6,0
S65W	56	Double Chts on a ridge
N20W	156	BO. Ct
S45E	116	2 Chts on a steep hill
N00E	40	tall Black O; on a hill by Huffs creek N side W
		Surd for John Mills on little Bottom Creek beg. a
WO on	ye N side of sd Creek thence	
S60W	58	tall WO
N60W	34	Chest on a Ridge
S50W	140	3 Chts by a Hollow
S15E	120	forked RO (run 40)
S70E	140	crossing Huffs Creeke to 2 W pines (Little Bottom Creek 40)
N50E	44	WO tree
N77E	210	3 pines in a grove corners to ye above mill place with sd line
N10W	110	to white pine on a Hill first corner of sd Place thence
N20W	70	W pine in Ingrams line 10 poles from his [illegible] with sd line
[illegible]	46	2 RO [illegible] thence to ye Beg. (Cr. 20)

29

Page 29

20th Feb'y 1753 - John Mill's Mill place.

7th March 1753 - Chesnut Noche on Huff's Creek.

Sur'd for John Mills on Little Bottom Creek - crossing Huff's Creek adj. Ingram's line.

2d March 1753 John Mills on Little Bottom Creek beg at a Burch & BO in Huffs Line & running thence
N 60 W 70 2 Chts. On a Rocky Hill.
S 25 W 00 WO & CHt
S 77 W 142 2 Wht Oaks on a bank of the Creek
S 25 W 64 2 Span: Oaks
N 60 W 36 crossing the Creek to a H. on y hill side

Rec'd

beg at a Cht. in a Valley by a Branch
N 25 E 134 — Sash trees by the Creek
N 50 E 100 to a Cht. on y Hill (Run 80)
S 77 E 120 H & Cht. on a Mountain
S 50 E 84 H & Cht. on a Spur
S 10 E 74 to WO BO corner to Leonard Huffs Land
S 75 W 52 to a Burch & BO y Beg of y above Land

5th March 1753 Martins Cove on Muddy Lick Creek
beg at 2 WO on y point of a Hill &
N 75 E 80 WO 2 BO } Protract
N 40 E 42 WO by a run }
S 75 E 152 Parcel of BO by a swamp
S --- 40 Lay WO
S 60 W 216 4 pines (run 200)
S 15 W 24 between 2 WO
S — W 40 between 3 WO by a Draft
West 50 — thence open:
N 9 Eight — 220 Acres
N 9 E 194

Roanoke Waters

Exam'd

Rec'd

30

Page 30

2nd March 1753 - John Mills on Little Bottom Creek adj. Huff's line.

[Another tract - no name given] - adj. Leonard Huff's line

5th March 1753 - Martin's Cave on Mudd Lick Creek - 220 acres. Roanoke waters.

****

Surveyed for Jnm Mc Adoo on Roanoke Waters beg
at 3 W O by a meadow thence

N 50 E 46 3 B O (upy run crossing)
N 85 E 42 2 B O on a Hill
N 30 E 112 3 Spt On a ridge
West 140 2 B O in a Hollow
S W 170 W O by the forkes of a run crossing the same at the foot of a mountain
6th march

N 45 E 146 to a pine on a ridge
N 60 W 56 B O,
N 80 W 156 2 B O
North 20 4 B O
West 178 2 W O & 2 B O in Monaghans Line & with the same
S 23 W 48 2 W O run 40 Monaghans corner & with his line
South 40 2 W O by a meadow under a hill along the run
210 — to the Beg 253 acres

Rec'd

Exam'd

11th March 1753 John Neely beg a buory tree by his Line on Catawba

S 70 W 144 tall B O in a Valley
S 15 E 82 B O by a Branch
S 70 E 50 B O & H in his line thence along to the beg
145 poles to the beginning
60 acres

Rec'd

Exam'd

A

31

Page 31

Surveyed for John McAdoo on Roanoke waters beg. By a meadow thence... adj. Monaghan's line - 253 acres.

11th March 1753 - John Neely - beg. A survey here by his line on Catawba - 80 acres

6th March | John Mills on Wolf Creek & falling Creek

\+ Beg at 3 B O s at ye Spur of a Mountain

S38W 50 Locust & B O
S70E 42 2 B O s
S10E 36 3 W O s
S55E 56 2 B O s
S10E 216 W O s in a glade (Wolf Creek 100 Burr 140
S70E 140 W O by a mountain
N30E 100 W O by a Spurr
East 80 2 B O s
S.E. 112 3 Chts on a Spurr
N6E 60 W O by ye Bank of a Branch
N60E 64 pine (Crank?)
N14W 164 2 W Os on ye side of ye ~~Little~~ Glade mountain (runs 54

Rec'd

Doctr Neely Beg at B O & 2 H corner to his Pat land
\+ & corner to Francis Neely Land thence
N70E 162 B O & 2 H s on a ridge
N10W 32 W O s in [illegible] Line of John McClenachan
N42W 54 B O H corner to sd Land thence
N65W 40 2 H s
S80W 106 2 W O B O s
S40W 52 1 W O B O Grubs by a Branch
S5W 28 to W O in his Line by sd Branch & with same
92 to ye Beg:
125 Examd 32

Rec'd

Page 32

8th May - John Mill's on Wolf Creek & Falling Creek Beg. At 3 B.O. at ye spur of a mountain ... on ye side of ye Glade Mountain. - 54 acres

Doct'r Meely [?] adj. His Pat. land & corner to Francis Realy land and John McClunaehan - 125 acres

****

Uriah Akers beg: @ 3 B O: in Tho Akers Pat Land & with s^d Line several courses about 40 Corners Passing 3 pines for one corner &c crossing Wolf Creek to 3 pines by a Glade & summit from thence

S 70 E 60 B O on a Hill to Wolf Creek 44 Rod
N 50 E 92 A s by a Glade in Mills Line & with ye same
N 10 W 348 to a B O on a Spur of the mountain thence
to ye Beg

to Be Joined with Mills Survey in his 348 pole Line

10th March 1753
Richd Kerr on Creely's Branch Roanoke: beg^g at
W O s corner to ye Land of Col^o Wood & with ye Land crossing ye Bran
S 83 E 18 W O & Sorrel wood corner to s^d Land
North 340 3 B O s
N 42 W 60 travel of Grubs
N 10 W 60 2 W O by a Branch
S 60 W 60 Crossing two branches to 3 B O s thence to ye Beg
South 226 & S 23 E 200 to ye Beginning
175 Acres

Exam^d

33

Page 33

Uriah Aker - Beg: at 3 BO in Tho's Aker's Pat. Land crossing Wolf Creek adj. Mill's line on his 348 pole line.

10th March 1753 - Rich'd Kerr on Creely's Branch Roanoke adj. Corner to ye land of Col. Wood - 75 acres

****

Wm Beard Begining at 3 Pines corner to ye Land of Thos Akers & with his New Line

S 70 E 60 BO on a hill Wolf Creek

N 50 E 92 crossing a Glade to a H in mett Line with sd Line

S 10 E - 12 WO in sd Glade and with ye Line of sd Land

S 70 E - 140 WO by a mountain

S E - - 100 pine on a Spurr

S 55 W 40 - Dou: Cht.

S 35 E - 110 BO by a Branch thence down

East 40 WO at ye forks of sd Branch

S 25 W 116 WO on a Spur

West 100 BO on a Ridge

N 13 W 12 - to a Lowst & Popplar corner to ye Land of Ann Armstrong & with her Line

N 41 E 84 WO by a Spring & with ye Line of sd Land

N 20 W 80 parcel of BOs

West 86 WO in a Glade } all with her Land Lines

N 5 W 136 2 WOs

S 61 W 26 crossing W Creek to BO on ye Bank

N 45 W 54 2 WOs by a Glad thence to ye beg

To Be Joined with Wm Beard

34.

Page 34

Wm. Beard - Beginning at 3 pines corner to ye land of Tho's Akers & with his new line on Wolf Creek adj. Mill's line , Ann Arnold [?].

****

2 March 1753 Sur John Thompson on Glade Creek beg at a
poplar on ye on a Hill south side of sd Creek corner to Hugh Mills & thence the same

NW 26 2 pines & WO in his corner
N37 E 100 4 pines on a Branch
N10 W 94 WO by ye Branch
N35 W 60 4 WO
N70 E 60 pine
S50 E 110 2 pines

Recd
Exam'd

S25 W 56 - - - - - - -
N71 W 32 2 pines WO corner to Col Woods Land } Protract S53 W 68 Poles
S10 W 60 crossing the Creek 3 WO corner to Thompsons Pat
Land thence Down by ye Beg 114 Poles 87 acres

Daniel Morrice beginning at a Potabuck on the Creek 20
N side of the same by ye bank thence up ye River
N30 E 70
N20 W 66
N55 W 20 2 Hicories by the mouth of Catawba
S5 E 88 WO by a sink hole
S60 W 52 2 WO on a Hill side along ye same 63 Poles to ye Beg
33 Acres

13th March 1753 Rec'd Exam'd

35

Page 35

3rd March 1753 - Sur'd John Thomson on Glade Creek, corner to Hugh Mills and Col. Wood's land - 87 acres.

13th March 1753 - Daniel Morrice beginning at a branch of the Creek, s[outh] side of the same by s'd bank thence up ye River [Catawba] - 33 acres.

****

12th ~~March~~ Ap: 1753
Wm Baird On both sides Back Creek a Branch of Roanoke beg at a WO on ye South side of the Creek
+ as Runeth thence Crossing the Creek —
N 10 E 80 B O W O on a Hill
West 40 2 pines Run 92
S.W. 50 W O on a Bank
South 60 crossing the Creek to a pine on a steep Bank
— -62 to Beg. 34 acres
Exam'd

13 ap: 1753
Wm Armstrong beg: at 2 W O & a B O on ye N side of Glade Creek High his own Patent Land
+ S 67 W 60 2 W O B O on a Hill side
S 5 E 65 W O in a Swamp in Monachans line
S 75 E 94 2 H & W O in a Glade
S 65 E 100 3 pines
N 80 E 54 4 B O
N W 100 2 B O in sd Armstrong's Pat line by his Barn
65 Acres not Recorded in my New Book
62 poles to the Beg
Exam,

36

Page 36

12th Ap. 1753 - Wm. Baird on both sides Back Creek, a branch of Roanoke beg.: at a W.O. on ye south side of the Creek & runeth thence crossing the Creek - 34 acres.

13 Ap: 1753 - Wm. Armstrong beg.: at 2 W.O. & a B.O on ye s[outh] side of Glade Creek, nigh his own patent land ... "in s'd Armstrong's pat. Line by his barn." - "65 acres not recorded in my new book."

****

Ress^r Millo & Miller on Milligan Branch beg. at a WO by a Spring head thence MILLIGAN

East 120 2 pines 2 WOs
S56 E 38 WO tree
East 40 3 WOs
S27 E 24 3 BO Grubs
S70 E 100 2 WO on ye Bank ...
S40 W 70 Hs
N80 W 140 WO
N40 W 60 nigh a chest Oake ...
S55 W 124 WO
N27 W 40 WO corner to ... with s^d same
West 40 WOs
N30 W 60 3 Hs in ...
N65 E 86 Locust
N25 W 90 2 WOs
N65 W 160 BO in the Barren
14th Apr. 1753
Capt. John Thomas on Dirty ... Bushes by ye spring head in a Gap of the Mountain
S50 W 72 WO in a Draft
S15 E 60 WO by a Run
S28 W 100 WO 3 BOs in a Valley ... Creek
S40 E 80 3 pines thence ... & then
to ye Beg.
N28 100 Pole along ye Mountain
X 170 to ye Beginn

37

Page 37

14th Ap.: 1753 - Mess'rs Mills & Miller on Milligan Branch. Beg.: at a W.O. by a spring head thence...

16th Ap.: - John Thomas on Dirty - - - 2 bushes by ye spring head in a gap of the mountain - near mouth of Glade Creek - 87 acres.

****

17th Ap: 1753 Alex.r Ingram beg at 2 B.O on the West side of a Draft of Runeth

S 35 E 44 Leaning WO
S 75 W 160 WO tree
N 35 W 60 WO B.O on the top of a Ridge to y.e Beg
+
54 acres

Exam.d
Rivers Recorded

17th Ap:
Sur. for Erwin Patterson beg: 3 B.O N. W. 4 R.o on a high bank on the North side of Roanoke opposite to his House thence
N 30 E 160 3 WO 2 BO (Rum 35)
S 50 E 320 BO WO in the Barrens Rec.d
South 90 3 BO on the Rivers Bank by 3 Indian Graves
N 69 W 350 to y.e beg 210 acres noted.
Exam.d

19th Ap: 1753 Surveyed for Ephraim Vause on the Ben Mountain on a Branch of Roanoke beg: at 2 Chest. & a BO at the foot of a Hill thence
North -- 100 3 Chest.s on a ridge crossing a Spring Branch
West -- 160 Chest. & BO by a Sink hole Rec.d
South 80 4 BO
S. W. 60 3 BO (Rum 36)
South 60 poles 2 WO (Rum 40)
S 80 W 100 Chest.
S 40 E 100 crossing a Branch to a Chest. a Spanish O. & Chest. on the side of a Hill the ... to y.e beg ...
310 poles along a mountain.

293 acres
Exam.d

38

Page 38

17th Ap.: 1753 - Alex'r Ingram beg.: nigh Jestoes Farry [sic] at 2 W.O. on the west side of a draft & runeth .. - 52 acres.

17th Ap.: Sur'd for Erwin Patterson b'g: 3 B.O. on N[orth] side of R'r [River] a high bank on the North side of Roanoke opposite to his house thence ... adj. 3 Indian Graves - 210 acres - not Re'd.

19th Ap.: 1753 - Surveyed for Ephraim Vause on the Bent Mountain on a branch of Roanoke beg.: at 2 ches't & a B.O. at the foot of ye hill thence ... 293 acres.

****

[illegible] April 1753 Sur.d for James Boyle beg.n at a BOWO[illegible] at the foot of a Hill thence
S 15 E 40 3[illegible] on the North side of y.e N Branch of Goose Creek and up the same
S 75 W 114 to a Walt. & H[illegible] on y.e Bank of s.d Creek by a Hill
North 40 to a pine & WO thence to y.e Beg: 28 Acres
106 to y.e Beg Recd Ex.d

27.th Ap: 1753 Thomas Bromeger beg at 3 pines on the West side of a Hill Exam.d Recd
N, W. 64 BOWOS
[illegible] W 80 [illegible] 3 pines in the Barrens
S, E, 86 2 W.O.S by a Draft of Meadow — Peter Dilles old Place 40 Acres
N 31 E 82 to y.e Beg

& Paul Simpson
28th Ap: 1753 John Donily on the Head Waters of Catawba a Place known by y.e name of the Knob beg at 2 Lynn's on the North side of a Hill thence
North 70 BOR on a Ridge
N, E, 260 Chest & Hickory
S 25 E 68 Ch.t & HO
S 10 W 60 Crossing the Creek to a Poplar & Locust thence [illegible] 245 poles to the Beginning
136 Acres Exam.d

Page 39

- - April 1753 - Sur'd for James Boyle. Beg.: at a B.O., W.O. at the foot of a hill thence... on the North side of ye North Branch of Goose Creek and up the same ... 28 acres.

27th Ap.: 1753 - Thomas Briniger - beg. At 3 pines on the west side of a hill - 3 pines in the barrins [sic] - Peter Dills old place. - 40 acres.

28th Ap: 1753 - John Donely & Paul Garrison on the head waters of Catawba at a place known by the name of the Knobs beg. At 2 lynn;s on the north side of a hill thence... 136 acres.

****

28th Ap: 1753 John Keighler beg at a forked WO corner to
Survey thence up N55E 60 poles 2WO.
N20E 86 2BOs on a Ridge
+ S,E, 40 crossing the creek to a pine thence
Down the same to the End of the Line that Remith from Sd forked WO
in this old Survey to be added in one Plan

Removed to new Book. Recd

Ann Armstrong beg at 2WO. on the West side of a hill
nigh Roanoke River thence
S25E 30 BO tree
East 60 WOH on a hill side Recd
N10E 54 Sp. Oak in the East Line of her first Survey
50 poles from the begining of the same which 50 poles
is to be struck out and the above Courses added into the
Survey

Nale McNale beg at a BO in the Barrens in
a Line of Mark Evans Land thence running
North 140 to 2BOs and a WO tree in Carvans old Patent Line & with
the same
N73W 150 to a Stake Sd Carvins Corner & with his Line
N55E 60 2 HGrubs WOs thence
N44E 174 WO by a Branch Recd
N34W 140 WO
S60W 116 H
S38W 140 WOH
S35E 26 to Mark Evans Line & with the same
S30E 345 to the begining 325 Acres
2d May 1753 not Recorded 40

Page 40

28th Ap.: 1753 - John Kighler beg. At a forked W.O. corner to - - - - survey thence up... "Down the same to the end of the line that runeth from s'd forked W.O. in his old survey to be added in one plan."
"Removed to new book - rec'd"

Ann Armstrong - beg. At 2 W.O. on the west side of a hill nigh Roanoke River thence. "...Sp'h [Spanish] oak in the east line of her first survey 50 poles from the beginning of the same which 50 poles is to be struck out and the above courses added in to the survey."

2nd May 1753 - Nale McNale - beg. At a B.O. in the barrens in a line of Mark Evans land thence...adj. Carvin's old patent line - 325 acres - not recorded.

****

3 of May 1753 John Patton beg at an Ash on ye North side of a Hill by a Spring thence
North 40 po: WO
N55 W 40 WO on a ridge
N10 E 44 WO on a Hill side
S70 E 146 3 H's
South 120 WO tree & H's on a Hill thence to the Beg.
124 Poles to ye beg 100 acres

Rec'd
Exam'd

(Run 41)

Wm Ralston beg at a BO on a Hill side nigh a Spring th:
S, E, 42 BO WO's on a hill
N, E, 46 BO
East 46 2 BO's by a Draft by a line of Mr Ralston's Land
North 24 BO by a run & West 65
along ye hill 100 poles to ye beginning

86 Acres

Exam'd Rec'd

Charles Milligon beg: at a Gum & Sp: O by a rocky hill
S, E, 42 3 WO's, BO's
N, E, 56 3 WO's by a Draft
West East 24 Chest:
N, E, 80 BO, H on a ridge
N15 W100 WO tree BO &c
3d May 1753

84 Acres

Rec'd

Page 41

3rd of May 1753 - John Patton - beg. At an ash on ye north side of a hill by a spring thence... - 100 acres.

Wm. Ralston - beg. At a B.O. on a hill side nigh a spring thence... adj. Jn'o Ralston's land - 36 acres

3rd May 1753 - Charles Milligan - beg: at a gum & Sp.O. [Spanish Oak] by a rocky hill - 84 acres.

****

29 ap: Wm Snodgrass beg at 3 H:s by a Draft — thence
S75 W 80 3 WO 1 H by a String.
S36 E 22. to Dr. Mitchells corner WO, & with his Line
S23 E 100 to a BO in sd Line thence
N 80 E 140 3 BOs by his Pat Line thence to ye beg:
82 Acres Recd

Wm Corrivan beg: at 2 BO & a WO tree in the line
of his Pat Land & corner to Hale McNeals Land thence
South 140 to BO in Evans Line & with ye same
S38 E 200 ~~3 WO &c &c thence~~
2 WO grubs in the Barrens
N60 E 160 3 WO & 2 H
N10 W 146 WO & 2 H on the side of a Hill Recd
N10 E 24 H & Locust by the Branch corner to the
old Survey made by Mr Poage & with the same the several
courses to the beg. (Reversed)
2d May 1753

42

Page 42

29 Ap.: - Wm. Snodgrass - beg. At 3 H's [hickory ?] by a draft thence - adj D'd Mitchells corner - 82 acres.

2nd May 1753 - Wm. Carrivan - beg: at 2 B.O. & a W.O. tree in the line of his Pat. Land & corner to Nale McNeal's land thence... adj. Evan's line in the barrens ... "by the Branch corner to the old survey made by Mr. Poage & with the same the several courses to the beg.: (reversed)."

****

James Elliot beg at 2 B O at ye foot of a Hill on the south side of Back creek & running thence

N 20 W. 20 to a W O on the bank of the creek

N 50 E 40 2 B O on a spur

N 30 E 54 double H in Lauderdales line & with the same

N 35 W 24 to his corner Poplar on a ridge & with s^d Line

N 75 E 84 3 W O his corner & with that Line

N 25 E 36 2 Hiccorys on a ridge then leaving his Line

S 80 E 20 to 2 B O & a W O Lukim Cherrys corner & with his Line

S 30 E 90 cross the creek to 2 W O. by a ~~Draft~~ Hiccory th: ~~to~~ Hiccory along a hill 217 poles to ye Beg

4th may 217 poles - 88 acres

Rec^d Exam^d

Exam^d

James Lauderdale beg at a B O on a Hill corner to his Patent Land on Loony's creek & runs thence

S 25 W 80 3 W O & B O

West 20

N 65 W 40 to a W O pop: & ash harbisons corner by ye Creek or N 71 E 56: Protract

N 50 W 140 cross ye creek to 2 W O

North 40 2 B O & H on a ridge nigh his Pat line

210 poles to ye Beg: Rec^d

4th may 85 acres

Page 43

4th May - James Elliot - beg. At 2 B.O. at ye foot of a hill on the south side of Back Creek & runneth thence... adj. Landerdale's line; Luke McCherry. 88 acres.

4th May - James Landerdale - beg. At a B.O. on a hill corner to his patent land on Loony's Creek & runs thence ...85 acres.... t a W.O. [,] pop. & ash harbisons** corner by ye creek N.[Nov.] 7, 1756.

** Should be Harbison's.

Col Patton nigh Robert Clerks Survey beg at a W O a glade and runs thence —

S, E, 114 Hiccory by Clerks Line (C)

S 25 E 70: 3 WO in the Head of a Hollow Rec'd

N 55 E 60: 2 pines

N 30 E 100 to 3 BOs on y Side of a Stony hill — Branch 80 running Eastward

S 82 W 250 to y Beg ------

5th may — 100 Acres — Exam'd

Henry Switcher beg at a WO BOs on y S. Side of Back Creek by the mouth of a hollow

N 50 W 100 3 WOs on a Ridge Cross y Creek

N 15 E 80 3 WOs

N 80 E 52 BO WO

S 65 E 100 cross the Creek to a Large BO on a hill — Creek 80

--- 136 poles to the Beg 85 Acres not Rd.

Exam'd

Hugh Carrothers beg a 2 WOs Lauderdales corner & with [illegible]

S 80 E 170 2 WO on a hill thence

N 20 E 140 BO tree

N 80 W 54 2 WOs by a run — Exam'd

S 40 W 96 BO

S 80 W 48 BO on a hill side by a run thence

--- 60 poles to y Beg:

86 acres not Rec'd

4th may

44

Page 44

5th May - Col. Patton nigh Robert Clerk's survey - beg. At a W.O. by a glade runs thence - 100 acres.

Henry Switcher - beg. At a W.O. & B.O. on the south side of Back Creek by the mouth of a hollow - 85 acres.

4th May - Hugh Carrothers - beg: at 2 W.O. - Landerdales corner with his line ... 86 acres.

****

James Lauderdale beg at 2 WO by ye foot of a hill corner to Hugh Carothers & with his Line
S 80 E 170 2 Hs on a ridge corner to Elliots Land & with his Lines
S 25 E 36 3 WO
S 75 W 04 pops on a ridge
S 35 W 90 popn by a Spring and Leaving Elliotts Line
S 75 W 60 WO tree
N 60 W 108 WO H
North 20 poles 2 Hiccories at the Head of a Hollow
& 142 poles along ye hill to ye Beg
143 acres Not Recd Exam

Luke McSherry beg: at 2 WOs on ye S side of back Creek corner to James Elliots Land & with his Line Cross the Creek
N 30 W 90 2 BO WO on a ridge
N 60 E 94 BO on a hill
North 30 2 WOs by a Spring
N 60 E 56 2 pines in the Head of a hollow
S 30 E 88 WO on a Steep bank
N 60 E 130 WO & ash by the Creek } Protracted & makes South 85 East 158 po:
S 30 E 42 cross the Creek WO BO on a hillside. thence
300 Poles up the Creek to the Beginning
5th May 1753 186 acres not Record. Exam

45

Page 45

James Landerdale - beg. At 2 W.O. by ye foot of a hill corner to Hugh Carothers & with his line ... adj. Corner to Elliot's land - 143 acres.

5th May 1753 - Luke McGherry - beg: at 2 W.O. on ye s[outh] side of Back Creek corner to James Elliot's land & with his line cross the creek... 186 acres - not record'd & exam'd

****

John Marshall beg at 2 W.O. (?) by a branch &c.
to the Line of his Pat Land & runs thence
S 46 W 70 3 WO by a ~~branch~~ (~~run 66~~)
S 5 W 140 2 W.O. on a Bank (run 66)
S 60 E 40 cross the run 3 WO by a Gully
N 20 E 60 3 W.O. on a Rocky hill
North 60 2 WO & H
N 20 E 80 4 W.O.
24 poles to ... 60 acres. Exam'd. Rec'd

8th may

Josiah Ramsay beg at 2 B.O. in Bordins Line & with the same
N 7 E 260 3 B O of said Line (run W 60
N 70 W 156 B O W O on a rocky hill — (run 100
S 60 W 52 W O on a Burr. Rec'd
S 17 E 150 an Ash in a Gully in a line of Davies Land (B 20
S 80 E 72 W O, by with sd Line ~~to ...~~ ~~...~~ poles
120 to the ...
160 acres ———

8th may 1753 Exam'd

100

Page 46

8th May - John Marshall - beg. At 2 Sp. O. & a H. By a branch to the line of his pat. Land & runs thence ... 60 acres

8th May 1753 - Josiah Ramsay - beg. At 2 B.O. in Bordin's line & with the same ... "in a gully in a line of Davies' land" - 160 acres.

****

James Davies beg at a Sp. O W O & H by a Bran
corner to another survey of sd Davies thence
S, W, 64 2 W O
South, 120 3 Pine sap. on a hill Record?
S 10 E 46 4 W O s by a run & Down y Same
S 80 E 34 B O W O in Bordins Line by a Branch & with
N 17 E 320 2 B O W O corner to the Land of Josiah sd Line
Ramsay & corner to a Line of his old survey & with
sd Line to the beg S.W. 126 poles
100 acres not Recd Exam
8th may 1753

on a Branch of Catawbo
9th may 1753 George Hollis, beg at 2 Sp: O s at the
Foot of a mountain thence
S 20 E 100 H B O (branch 60)
South 70 W O by a run Exam:
S, E, 62 2 B O
S, W 100 2 Sp: O s on a ridge Branch 20
N 35 W 100 Large B O at ye head of a hollow nigh the
along the mountain 160 poles to ye Beging mountain
144 acres Not Recorded

47

Page 47

8th May 1753 - James Davies - beg. At a Sp. O & W.O. & H by a barn corner to another survey of s'd Davies thence... adj. Bordin's line, corner to the land of Josiah Ramsay & corner to a line of his old survey - 100 acres.

9th May 1753 - George Hollis - be. On a branch of Catawba at 2 Sp. O at the foot of a mountain thence.... - 144 acres.

****

James Hollis beg at S.W. Corner to one Tract of Land and runs th Thence with Ramsays Line
N 80 E 100 [illegible]
S 25 E 86 [illegible] Locust
S 60 W 116 Locust in a hollow
S 25 E 104 WO on a rocky hill
S 40 W 176 2 WO on a ridge Examd
West 100 WO
N 30 W 132 WO in a Line of Burdens Land & with the same to ye beg
9th may 312 poles to the Beg:
— 395 Acres not Rec'd

John Marshall beg at a RBOs in a Line of his Land
N, E, 120 Parcel of Oak Sap:
N 55 W 84 2WO
S 65 W 140 Span: O & pine Sap:
S 20 W 80 WO on a Bank
S 40 W 16 WOBOs in a valley corner to his Old Land thence by [illegible]
9th may 1753 1[illegible]4 poles to the Beginning
120 Acres Examd
Record

48

Page 48

9th May - James Hollis - beg. At 3 H's corner to one tract of - - - land and runeth thence with Ramsay's line - adj Bordin's land - 395 acres.

9th May 1753 - John Marshall - beg. At a H. B.O. in a line of his land ... in a valley corner to his s'd land thence. 120 acres.

****

Thomas Ramsay beg: at a Sp. O. & H including [illegible]
Land & ~~[illegible]~~
corner to the Land of Wm Hais thence
S, E, 38 with Bordins Line to his corner 3 W. Os with Halls Line
N 80 E 100 to his Corner tall 130
N 55 E 72 2 Ches[ts] a Line of sd Ramsays Land with the same
N 33 E 80 to his corner Cht & the same Course 160 po: W. O. on ridge
S 65 E 60 Sp: O in a Hollow
N 5 E 100 W O H by a Sink hole
S 75 W 34 2 R O[s]
N 65 W 44 H on a ridge
North 60 B O & Sp: O
N 70 W 50 B O on a Steep bank
N 35 W 20 to M Ferrins Corner by Lapsleys Run & the same course 48 poles B O in a hollow
S 40 W 126 H by Hais corner 3 W O & with his Line
S, E, 142 ash White Walnut in a Bottom Hais Corner (B 56

Recd 8
~~250~~ Acres
310 24th May
Exam[d]

13th June 1753 John Hargas on ye Short hill beg at a [illegible]
2 Chesnut Oaks on ye S Side of Branch & Cross the same
N.W. 44 Ches[t] on a hill th:
S.W. 190 2 Ches[ts] on a Spur
S 37 W 400 2 Chesnut Oaks
S, E, 60 Cross the Creek to 2 Pines on a mountain along
225 Acres (4th June 592 po: to ye Beg[n]

Recd Exam[d] 6

49

Page 49

10th May - Thomas Ramsay - beg. At a Sp.O [Spanish Oak] & H. [Hickory] In a line of - - - land corner to the land of John Har's thence... ajd. Bordin's line to his corner 3 H's & with Hollis line, McFerrin's corner by Lasseley's Run. 310 acres.

13th June 1753 - John Hargas on ye Short Hill beg. At 2 chesnut [chestnut] oaks on the s[outh] side of Branch & cross the same... 225 acres.

****

13th May 1753 Col° Pattons upper tract on ye [illegible]
James River Call'd Jennings Bottom, beg at 2 W O by ye [illegible]
Mountain thence
North 24 poles to 2 poplars by ye Bank of ye River & up the same
+ N70W 120, N.W 68; N20W 84, S.W. 82, South 54 po:
S35E 120, South 48 po: SE 30 to ye Elk Creek & up the same
N60E 76, S.E. 26 : Examd & Recd 243
East 50 } to Protract up ye River
S35E 78
S20W 40 wobo on ye Bank.
N10W 165 to ye Beg
~~N 30 E~~ on a hill thence to ye Beg [illegible] Acres

Col° Pattons Lower Survey on Jennings Bottom beg at a
WO & maple by the foot of a Mountain Runeth thence
N70W 24 to 2 WO on ye Rivers Bank So Side thence down
+ N15 E 60
N 20W 40
North 140
N20W140
N E 80 Spanish Oak on the Bank
S30 E 80 WO
40
Examd Recd

13th May 1753 176 Acres
along the Mountain 300 poles to a WO
S.W. 90 to ye Beg

50

Page 50

13th May 1753 - Col'o Patton upper tract on ye - - - James River, Col'd Jennings Owens - beg. At 2 B.O. by ye mountain thence ... Elk Creek - 243 acres.

13th May 1753 - Col'o Patton's lower survey on Jening's Bottom - beg. At a W.O. & Maple by the foot of a mountain runeth thence - near River Bank. - 176 acres.

****

Augst 50 Captain Smith on ye S. Side James River
beg: at a WO on the Bank thence up ye River

N 50 W 62
N 70 W 30
S 60 W 40
S 15 W 34
S 25 E. 100
S 35 E 40 BO by the Bank along ye River to ye Beg:
306

Recd
Exam'd

75 Acres

Colo Patton below Purgotory on ye North side James River
begining at a Locust on a hill side thence
N 70 E 30 to a Spanish Oak by ye River Bank thence up ye Sam
S 25 E 160
S 10 E 40
South 40
S 35 W 60
S 60 W 60 to 3 Ps. by ye River Opposite to a high Mountain
360
thence to ye [illegible]
N 3[illegible] W
[illegible] 3 W 295 to ye Beg

Recd Exam'd

125 Acres

51

Page 51

- - May 1753 - Captain Smith on the s[outh] side James River - beg. At a W.O. on the bank thence up s'd River - 75 acres.

Col'o Patton below Purgotory on the north side James River begining [sic] at a locust on a hill side thence ...opposite to a high mountain - 125 acres.

****

Alexr Walker on Broad Creek forks of James River
beg: at a Sugartree at the foot of a hill corner to the
Land of John Beaty and with his Line
N 40 W 114 to his two BO.
N 70 W 20 2 BOs
S 70 W 136 Hicory
North 80 WO on a hill
N 50 E 50 WO
S 60 E 52 RO
East 186 BO
S 60 WO by ye foot of a hill by the Creek ~~[illegible]~~
along ye hill 130 Poles to ye Beg:
14th June 1753
154 Acres

Recd ye Exam

David Miller on Fineys Run beg: at 2 WOs corner to Sd Gathier Land
S 75 E 100 to 2 Hs by a Branch
N 20 E 60 2 [illegible] by a Mountain
N 10 W 54 H WO
West 34 HWOs
N 15 E 46 HWOs
S 70 W 100 WO in Gathiers Line & with the same 98 to the Beg
19th Sept 1753 82 Acres

52

Page 52

14th June 1753 - Alex'r Walker on Broad Creek fork of James River - beg. At a sugertree at the foot of a hill corner to the land of John Beaty and with his line... - 154 acres.

19th Sep't 1753 - David Miller on Finey's Run - beg. At 2 W.O. corner to Ja's Gathiver land - 82 acres.

****

Sepr 1753
George Robinson beg 2 W O corner to Edward McDonalds Land (and in a Line of his own Pat Line
S 25 W 124 2 W O/ Chen David Robinsons Line & with ye same
East 140 2 W O/ & W O/ in Ed McDonalds Line & with the same
N 38 W 144 to ye Beg: 50 Acres
to the Beg:

18th Sepr 1753 John Neelys additional survey beg at the Second corner to ye first survey & runs thence
S 70 W 90 W O by a Draft
S 10 E 52 W O on a ridge
S 35 E 216 W O
N 60 E 80 2 W O
N 10 E 60 Double Ch^t thence a straight Line to where the former survey Ended in Neelys Line & with the same &c.
Then Added 220 Acres
Rec^d Ed

Surveyed for Bryan McDonnald on ye Waters of Roanoke Beginning at a Chest^t corner to his Pat Land & runs thence with a Line of Dr Mitchels Land
N 75 E 60 2 Ch^s
S 40 E 270 2 W O/ in Snodgrass's Line & with the same
S 60 W 120 W O W O in a Line of s^d McDonalds Land & with the same to the Beginning 150 Acres
27th Sepr 1753

Page 53

- - Sep't 1753 - George Robinson - beg. 2 W.O. corner to Edward McDonald's land and in a line of his own Pat. Line - adj. David Robinson's line - 50 acres.

18th Sep't 1753 - John Neely's additional survey - beg. A B.O. Second corner to ye first survey & runs thence... 220 acres.

27th Sep't 1753 - Survey'd for Bryan McDonnald on ye Waters of Roanoke - begining [sic] at a chest. [chestnut] corner to his Pat. Land & runeth thence with a line of D'd Mitchels' land - adj. Snodgrass's line - 150 acres.

****

23 Sept 1753
Surveyed for Aaron Hart on Roanoke Waters
Beginning WO & Popler at the Foot of a Ridge thence
N25E 60 WO
N35W 50 WO BO — 197 Acres
N65W 60 WO
S65W 40 BO
N60W 92 2 BO
S40W 68 2 BO by a Branch thence
S30E 200 2 WO at the Head of a Hollow & Down
the same to the Beg:

9th Sept 1753
Surveyed for John Clyde on Waters of [illegible]
[illegible] on a hill corner to [illegible]
[illegible]
North [illegible]
N60W [illegible] 2 Sp[illegible]
S80W 60 [illegible]
N30W [illegible] WO
S50W 120 [illegible] on a Branch
S30E 40 [illegible] on a high Ridge & along
the same to the Beg:
200 Acres

Page 54

23rd Sep'r 1753 - Surveyed for Aaron Hart on Roanoke waters - beginning W.O. & poplar at the foot of a ridge thence...

27th Sep'r 1753 - Surveyed for John Clyde on ye waters of Catawba - 200 acres.

****

[illegible] 1753 Surveyed for David Robinson
[illegible] Branch of Sinkers Creek beg: at 3 Hs 130 poles
to sd Robinson's Pat. Land thence
S10 E 152 2 Hs by a branch
S40 W 52 WO by a Branch & X the same
S35 E 80 SpO
N55 E 80 WO
North 200 WO by the above sd Line & with the same
to the Beg — 135 Acres

[illegible] Brezillah Reeves on the Waters of Roanoke beg at
2 Pt corner to Dd Mitchells Land thence
S40 E 80 RO P
N50 E 80 3 WO Branch 60
N10 W 180 3 Hs on a ridge
N60 W 60 RO
S40 W 80 2 BO
South 40 to 2 WO corner to sd Mitchells Land & with
his Line to the Beg 100 poles 143 Acres
1st October 1753

Page 55

- - Sep'r 1753 - Surveyed for David Robinson a branch of Tinker's Creek - beg. At 3 H's & B.O. corner to s'd Robinson's pat. land thence... 135 acres.

1 October 1753 - Brezillah Reeves on ye waters of Roanoke - beg. At 2 H's corner to D'd Mitchell's land thence - 143 acres.

Nr 1st 1752 Mr Wm Lredgrass his Addition

beg: at Dr Mitchells corner WO mentioned by the former survey & thence with his Line

S76 W 106 X a Branch HWO & Leaving sd Line

N22 E 60 to a BO

N63 W 42 2WO

N40 E 66 Large Popr

N70 E 120 X the sd Branch in the Line of ye former survey

at 2WO / about 20 poles from ye Begining Corner

David Miller beg at a Chtt & WO in Bryan McDonalds Line thence

N60 W 116 2BO under ye Mountain

+N.E. 68 2BO in a Line of Wood Land with the Line

S 8 E 200 BOWO his Corner

N37 E 24 BO &

S20 E 60 to a Cht Corner to sd McDonalds Land &c

194 Poles with his Line to the Beg

120 Acres

2d Octr 1753

Page 56

Oct'r 1 1753 - Wm. Snodgrass his additional - - - beg. At D'd Mitchell's corner W.O. mentioned & the former survey & thence with hi line...

2nd Oct'r 1753 - David Miller - beg. At a Cht. & W.O. in Bryan McDonald's line thence - 120 acres.

Oct. 1753 HEVIN. KEN[illegible]

Roanoke Water

[illegible] Roanoke [illegible]

N 60 W 100 WO beg. on BO in his Pat. line

N 10 E 104 WO

North 100 - [illegible] 144 Acres

East 40 - 2 BO

S 5 E 84 3 WO on a [illegible] hill

S 71 E 12 WO [illegible]

[illegible]

[illegible] George Robinson beg at a WO Sycamore corner to his old survey [illegible]

N 60 W 20. 3 BO

N 10 E 104 3 WO

North 100 BO [illegible]

West 60 WO in a [illegible]

South 200 2 WO [illegible]

S 62 E 18 [illegible] Pat. Line of Jos. McDonald

S 15 E 110 through the [illegible]

[illegible]

57

Page 57

Oct'r 1753 - Survey for Hevin Renfro on Roanoke water - beg. At B.O. in his pat. Line - 144 acres.

George Robinson - beg. At a W.O. & sycomore corner to his old survey - adj. Pat. Line of Jos. McDonald

****

Oct, 1753
22d Oct 1753 Surveyed for Archelas Willson on the Cowpasture River beg at 2 WO by a gully on N side River thence
Cow pasture River

+ S,E, 40 X y Creek WO by a Hill thence down y same
S 40 W 62
S 20 W 60
S 40 W 62
S 15 W 140 to a great pine at y foot of a Hill thence X y Ck
N,W, 40 2 pines

Wm Carlile beg 2 pines corner to Willsons Land & with y same
+ S,E, 40 X y Ck to a great pine thence down
S 30 W 400 to a pine by y foot of a hill thence
N W 40 2 WO on a hill side

Archlas Willson beg at 2 WO corner to Carlile with y same
+ S,E, 40 X y Branch to a pine thence down the same
S 30 W 120
S 5 W 80
S 40 E 26
S 30 W 120 WO thence X y River End
N 20 W 50 2 WO

58

Page 58

- - Oct'r 1753 - Survey for Archilas Willson on Cowpasture River - beg. At 2 W.O. by a gully on w[est] side Rier thence ...

Wm. Carolile - beg. 2 pines corner to Willson land & with ye same...

Archlas Willson - beg. At 2 W.O. corner to Carrolile's with ye same...

****

Jno. Lockridge on a branch of ye Great River of
the Calfpasture Beg at a W O by a Dft in ye Mountain on Calfpasture
West 60 W O ...s in a hollow
+ South 60 ... on a ... a high spurr
East 60 Ch... on ye point of a Rocky hill
North 60 to the Beginning 22 Acres
23d Octr. 1753

Jno. for ... Snodrass on the Waters of Cowtabo Beg at
3 H... by a draft and runneth thence
S 75 W 20 ... in a Draft and
N 63 W 140 Large Pop...
S 40 W 66 ... 2 W O
S 63 E 42 B O
S 22 W 60 R W O in Mitchells Line & with the same
N 76 E 106 to his corner W O, & with sd Line
S 13 E 100 Poles to a B O in sd line & leaving the same
N 80 E 140 3 ... W O ... Snodgrass Line thence
152 Poles to the Beg

1 Octr 1753

Left home on tuesday ... of Octr. 1753

59

Page 59

23rd Oct'r 1753 - - - - Lockridge on a branch of ye Great River of the Calfpasture - beg. At a B.O. by a dpt. In ye mountain - 22 acres.

1 Oct'r 1753 - Surv'd for Wm. Snodgrass on the waters of Cawtabo [Catawba] - beg. at 3 H's by a draft and runneth thence...adj. Mitchell's line.

"Left home on Tuesday 3rd of Dec'r 1753."

****

5th Dec. 1753 Surd. for [John] Harris [four] for[k] [of] James River Joining the Land of John Mathews [Matthews] at B.O. Hic. [corner] to sd Land & with his Lines

Ed Rd.

S 30 E 40 2 W.O.
S, W 60 130
+ S, E 65 Large W.O near a branch — 145 Acres
N 30 E 154 Walnut
N 70 E 26 2 W.O.s then leaving sd Lines
S 20 E 40 Hic.s on a hill
S, W. — 200 up a branch to 2 W.O.s in the Barrens &
N 75 W 156 to a W.O & Locust & Hic. [corner] on a Hill in a Line of
John Mathews Land & with the same 200 to the Beg

NOBLE

6th Decr. 1753 Surveyed for John Noble in the Fork of James River beg at a W.O on a hill on the South side [illegible] & thence running
+
S 65 W 60 130
S 35 W 140 Double Walt. — 120 Acres
S 30 E 60 SO
S 70 E 60 130 W.O.s
N 35 E 150 Large Poplar on a Ridge thence 93 Poles along the hill to the Beg

Ed Rd

60

Page 60

3rd Nov'r 1753 - Sur'd for John Berrisford on James River joing [sic] the land of John Matthews in the barrens. 145 acres.

6th Dec'r 1753 - Surveyed for John Noble in the Fork of James River - beg. At a W.O. on a hill on the south side Buffalo & thence runneth. 120 acres.

[illegible] 1753 [illegible] [illegible] M^c^Matthews in the Fork FORK
of [illegible] River beg at a BOWO corner to his Land & with [illegible]
JAMES
East 30 to BO then leaving his Line
North 28 Poles 3 WO
West 54 WO in M^c^Clures Line & with the same
S 35 W 60 WOBO M^c^Clures ~~his~~ Corner & with that Line
N 30 W 134 BO by the Road
S 50 W 116 WOBO
S 35 E 40 2 WO
S 25 E 46 WO corner to the Land of Geo Mathews & with [illegible]
[illegible] E 76 to WO corner to Richd Mathews & with his Line
S 65 E 110 H BO &
[illegible] W 20 BO and
[illegible] 5 56 to the Beginning

Ex^d^ Ro 100 Acres

Saml M^c^Roberts beg at BOWO corner to the Tract
on which he Lives & corner to James Hutchisons Land &
with his Line
South 120 Poles to a double Walnut & thence
S 60 E 60 Large Spanish Oak
N 50 E 140 H
N 40 W 54 WO by a Sink hole
N 75 W 90 WO on a ridge ~~by~~ a Line of S^m^ M^c^Roberts Land
& with the same 40 Poles to the Beg. — Ex^d^ Ro
12th Decr 1753

100 Acres
15 July 1751

61

Page 61

- - - Dec'r 1753 - Sur'd for Rich'd Matthews at the fork James River - beg. At a B.O. & W.O. on a corner to his land & with ye line.... adj. McClure and Geo'r Mathews. 100 acres.

12th Dec'r 1753 - Sam'l McRoberts - beg. at B.O. & W.O. corner to the tract on which he lives & corner to James Hutchison's land & with his line... - 100 acres 15 July 1754. [Note: both dates are given.]

5th Dec. 1753 Sur for Lukes McCherry ... Creek at WO on a barren Ridge thence — 60 acres

N50 W40 2WO corner to his old Survey thence

S25 W116 x ye South Branch of sd Creek to a WO on the Bank

S W 60 up ye Branch to 4 pines on a steep Bank — thence up — Ex'd

S50 E60 x ye same to a double poplar & WO

N E 60 to a WO Grub thence to the Beg (Not actualy Run)

Do. James Lauderdale beg at 2 WO at ye foot of a hill on ye S side of Back Creek corner to James Elliot & with his Lines

N20 W20 WO on a bank

N50 E40 2 WO on a spurr

N30 E54 Doublet [illegible] in a Line of sd Lauderdale's former survey

S35 E60 2 popr by a spring thence & with the same

S75 W60 WO tree

N60 W108 WO [illegible] then leaving sd Line

S30 W100 to 2 pines on ye N side of a hill by the Head spring of Back Creek & along sd hill to the Beg

15th Do. Surd for Andw McNeely beg at 4 WO's in his Line by a Branch of Looneys Creek under a hill thence — Ex'd

S75 E130 Cross the Branch to a WO in Wm Harbenson's Line thence with the same

North 80 ... poles

N75 W120 to a Parcel of Pines in sd McNeely's Line 80 Poles & with the same to ...

60 acres 62 [illegible]

Page 62

13th Dec'r 1753 - Sur. For Luke McCherry on ye - - - Creek at W.O. on a barren ridge thence... corner to his old survey thence... - 60 acres.

Do [13th Dec'r 1753] - James Landerdale - beg. at 2 B.O. at ye foot of a hill on ye s[outh] side of Back Creek corner to James Elliot & with hi lines ... "in a line of s'd Landerdale's former survey..." "To 2 pines on s'd n[orth] side of a hill by the head spring of Back Creek & allong s'd hill to the beg." - 60 acres.

15th Do [Dec. 1753] - Sur'd for And'w McNeely beg. At 4 W.O. in his line by a branch of Loonies Creek under a hill thence... cross the Branch to a W.O. in Wm. Harbison's line thence with the same. - 62 acres

****

Margrett
[illegible] Sloan beg at a WO in a Line of her Pat Land then
N70 W 36 2WO in James Sloans Line & thence
S14 W 54 X y Branch BO on a Barren hill by y Great Road
+ S70 E 70 WO BO by s Road in her Line & with y same to
y Beg
15th Dec 1753 Ed Red 18 Acres

James Lawderdale beg at a BO on a hill on y S Side a Stony
brick corner to his Pat Land thence
S25 W 80 Poles 3WO 1BO thence
S18 W 26 2WO 150 Acres
+ S75 W 70 2WO in a Line of Harbinsons Land & with y same
N21 E 120 X y Creek to a Stake thence (here I suppose I have made
a mistake by not runing a South course of 100 poles
West 160 2WO leaving harbinsons Lines
N50 W 60 3WO on a hill
N40 E 75 Spanish O: in a Line of his Pat Land 280 to y Beg Red Ed 150 Acres
15th Dec 1753 (So: 100 WO BO S th: S20 W 12, 2WO in y Line & with same)

John Bradley beg at a WO by a Branch in Harbinsons Line
N75 W 54 to WO in y Barren
+ S75 W 120 between 2WO
South
S74 WO on a ridge (or South)
N75 E 60 WO in widow Sloans Line 100 Acres
N25 E 38 WO on a hill * 38 poles only Red Ed
East - 90 3WO in a hollow in harbinsons Line & with
the same 110 Poles to y Beg
9 Dec 1753 63

Page 63

- - Nov'r 1753 - - - -on Sloan - beg. At a W.O. in a line of his pat. land thence... adj. "...ye branch B.O. on a barren hill by ye Great Road. - 18 acres.

15th Dec'r 1753 - James Landerdale by at a B.O. on a hill on ye s[outh] side Loony Creek souh [sic] corner to his pat. land thence... "ye creek to a stake thence (here I supose I have made a mistake by not runing a south course of 100 poles" - leaving Harbison's one corner - 150 acres

15th Dec'r 1753 - John Bradley - beg. At a W.O. by a branch in Harbinson's line - adj. Widow Sloan's line - 100 acres.

****

21st Decr. 1753

Surveyd for Thomas Lee on the Head of a Bran[illegible] Creek beg a 2 WO. at the Foot of a ridge thence —

S 5 E 86 2 H[illegible] in a hollow

East 80 Lin[illegible] WO by a Branch — Recd Ed

+ N 70 E 80 an ash in a hollow — 140 Acres

N 35 E 100 HWO[illegible]

N 5 W 60 2 WO on a Ridge & along the same 233 poles to the Beg

Do. Ann Patton beg at 2 WO. on the north side of Johns Creek corner to Jacob Patton & henry Holstor thence Runs

N 25 W 80 3 WO. — 70 Acres Recd Ed

S 70 W 160 - 3 pines

S 15 E — 60 to a Spruce pine on y Bank of sd Creek thence Down & crossing the same several times to the Beg

22d Decr. 1753 Surveyd for Frederick Hartsough beging at a pine & B O on a Hill side on y N Side of Mill Creek a branch of Craigs Creek thence

+ S 10 E 40 + y Branch to WO — 184 Acres Recd Ed

N 80 E 260 to a pine on a high Bank of Craigs Creek

N 15 E - 40 + sd Creek to a Locust corner to John Lowrys Land & with his Line

S 70 E 160 passing his Corner WO - to a pine

N 53 E 20 to a gum on the Bank of the Creek

N 55 W 200 up & cross the Creek thence a Streight Course 310 poles to the Beg

64

Page 64

21st Dec'r 1753 - Survey'd for Thomas Lee on the head of a branch - - - Creek - beg. - a 2 W.O. at the foot of a ridge thence... - 140 acres.

Ann Patton - beg.- at 2 B.O. on the north side of John's Creek corner to Jacob Patton & Henry Holston thence runs... - 70 acres.

22nd Dec'r 1753 - Survey'd for Frederick Hartsough - beging [sic] at a pine & B.O. on a hill side on ye w[est] side of Mill Creek a branch of Craig's Creek thence... "...corner to John Lowry's land..." - 18 acres.

****

[illegible] 175[illegible] [illegible] [illegible]

[illegible] Begin[illegible] [illegible] O W[illegible] corner CORNER

[illegible] of James Davies [illegible] with s^d Davies Line

JAMES DAVIES

[illegible] 64 2 WO

South 120 3 pines on a hill

S 10 E 46 [illegible] by a [illegible] then Leaving s^d Davies Line

S.W. 40 3 WO[illegible]

[illegible] 75 W 50 to a pine in Marshall's Line & with the same

[illegible] 55 W 60 2 WO[illegible]

S 6 W 90 [illegible] Leaving [illegible] Line N 20 W 40 WO [illegible]

[illegible] 55 W 64 2 WO

[illegible] 70 W 100 WO

[illegible] 75 W 40 WO

North 94 2 WO

East 58 3 pines corner to [illegible] Pat Land & with the same

S 29 E 60 2 WO

N 75 E 173 cross a Branch WO

N 5 W 80 WO[illegible]

N 14 E 56 3 WO

N 61 E 80 2 WO

N 28 E 40 2 WO

*S 50 E 40 WO then Leaving s^d Patent Line (*first set Down N 50 W 40)

N 70 E 40 WO by a branch [illegible] the same

East 42 to the Beginning

270 Acres

65

Page 65

- - - 1753 - Sur'd for Henry Swekhard - - - where he now lives - Beg. At 2 Spanish O & W.O. & H. corner to land of James Davies & runs thence with s'd Davies line... "to a line in Marshall's line & with the same..." - 270 acres.

****

26th Dec. 1753 ... [illegible]
nigh a Run by the foot of a steep Ridge ... [illegible]
Burdens Land on Catawba & runs thence
N40W 60 2WO on a point of a hill
North 32 WO Cross a branch
N26W 132 WO
N40E 60 Double Mulberry by a branch [illegible]
S26E 48 BO
S5 E 46 WO
S26E 120 WO
N60E 60 3 pines
N10W 80 WO
N70E 60 X branch to 2WO
S, E, 66 WO pine
N65E 26 WO by ... corner to ... Land [illegible]
S75E 80 3WO by a branch (to ... WO 40)
S26E 60 WO
S 80 W 40 BOWO by a branch corner to ... Borden
Line & corner to John Marshalls Land & with ... Line a Streight course 205 Poles to the Beginning

235 Acres

Rec'd Ex'd

Page 66

26th Dec'r 1753 - Sur'd for Josiah Ramsay - beg. Nigh a River by the foot of a Steep Ridge in a line of Bordin's land on Catawbo & runs thence... "by a W.O. corner to Swekhard's land..."..."by a branch corner to s'd Bordin's line & corner to John Marshall's land & with Bordin's line a ye height corner 205 poles to the beginning." - 235 acres

****

[illegible] beg at 2 W O s at the Foot of a Mount
[illegible] Waters of Glade Creek a Branch of Roanoke
N 70 W 66 W O on a point of a Ridge by a Branch
N 10 E 160 B O
+ N 40 E 130 2 W O Grubs on a Rich hill   Rec'd Ex'd
S 70 E 100 3 Pines Fall of S'd Mountain Foot & along
29th Dec'r 1753 the same 280 to the Beginning 165 Acres

Nathan Nicholas beg at a poplar on a hill side on the
West side of a Branch of Glade Creek then Down
+ S 25 E 140 H, B O,
N 65 E 40 + s'd Branch W O & pine   Rec'd Ex'd
N 25 W 100 Spanish Oak & H   54 Acres
N 65 E 80 W O
N 25 W 40 B O on a Spur of S'd Mountain & along s'd same
31 Dec'r 1753 S 65 W no to the Beginning

10 Jan'y 1754 Surv'd for Fredrick Shore beg at 2 W O by the Bank on the W't side woods River thence Down the same
N 85 E 106
S 75 E 60   80 Acres
+ S, E 64
S 33 E 78 Double W O [illegible] on the Bank thence
N, E, 54. 2 pines by a Meadow   Rec'd Ex'd
N 75 E 26 W O by a Spring thence ~~to the Beg~~
N 60 W 192
S 64 W 119 [illegible]
South 30 Poles to the Beg

67

Page 67

2nd Dec'4 1753 - ___rd Reed - beg. at 2 B.O. at the foot of a mountain of ye waters of Glade Creek, a branch of Roanoke...

31 Dec'r 1753 - Nathan Nicholas - beg. at a poplar on a hill side on the west side of a branch of Glade Creek thence down... - 54 acres.

10 Jan'y 1754 - Sur'd for Fredrick Shore - beg. at 2 H's by the bank on the west side Wood's River thence down the same... - 80 acres.

Surd for Phillip Harris on a North Branch of Creek beg at a Large WO by a guley at the foot of a hill
N,E, 60 2 Sp: O
N,W, 60 X a Branch 2 RO — 130 Acres
S 60 W 160 2 WO in a hollow
S 30 W 142 Parcel of WO by a Sink hole — Rec'd Ex'd
S,E, 50 X y Branch 2 WO under a Rockey hill thence
230 Poles to y Beg.
30th Jany 1754

16th Feby 1754 Resurveyed for George Reid Adam Lydays Land Beg at a WO on a hill ... of y B Branch Roanoke
N 38 W 40 WO in Sharkeys Line & with the same
S 52 W 76 to his Corner 2 WO. thence with his Line
N 38 W 40 X y Ck to a B O
S 60 W 186 WO on a hill side (the Land there 130 & 50 poles Wide)
S 50 W 160 2 H S by sd Ck
S 67 W 60 2 WO on a Rocky hill
S,W, — 60 Walt S in Cyphers Line & with the same
S,E, — 60 X y Ck to a Spanish Oak on a hill thence ~~.....~~
520 ~~...~~ to y Beg
204 Acres in all — Rec'd Ex'd
(formerly 104 acres)

68

Page 68

30th Jan'y 1754 - Sur'd for Phillip Harless on a North Branch of - - - Creek - beg. At a large W.O. by a guly at the foot of a hill - - - -... - 130 acres.

16th Feb'y 1754 - Surveyed for George Reed , Adam Lydass land - beg. At a W.O. on a hill w[est] side of ye branch Roanoke - "...in Sharkey's line & with the same..." - "..W[alnut] at Jim Cyphers' line & with the same..." - 204 acre in all (formerly 104 acres).

... Garrison Beg at a Ch^t. & B O Corner to the L
on which he now Dwells & with his Line
S 10 W 60 x ye Branch to a poplar & Locust then down
S 55 E 50 to 4 Lyns under a hill
N 75 E 64 x ye Branch to a Sp: O 33 Acres
North 20 to a B O by the Knob thence to ye Beg.
16th Feby 1754 Ex^d Rec^d

D^o John Donily Beg 3 Ch^ts on ye S. side of a hill Ridge
on ye head of Calebons thence
S 20 E 36 2 L^ts in a hollow 35
N 70 E 80 3 W O^s Rec^d Exam^d
N, E, 60 + a B^h to 2 W O^s in the Forks of s^d Branch
N, W, 40 to a P on the Ridge & along the same

Robt Brown beg at 3 W O on ye S side Peters Creek
N 56 E 192 W O in ye Barrens
N 34 W 100 3 W O^s
S 30 W 60 2 W O^s by ye Creek 115 Acres
West 20 + ye Ch to a Double W O
N, W, 50 2 B O^s 166 pole
S 56 W 54 W O in a hollow & along ye hill to ye Beg
25th Feby 1754 Rec^d Ex^d

69

Page 69

16th Feb'y 1754 - - - - Garrison - beg. At a Chest & B.O. corner to the land on which he now dwells & with his line ... near the Knobs - 33 acres.

16th Feb'y 1754 - John Donely - Beg. - 3 Chests. On ye s[outh] side of a hill ridge on ye head of Catabow thence... - 36 acres.

25th Feb'y 1754 - Rob't Brown - beg. At 3 W.O. on ye s[outh] side Peters Creek near the barrens - 115 acres.

****

23.d Feby 1754

on which he lives ... two ...

the foot of a hill nigh a Branch of ... Goose Creek
Then ... ... the Creek

North 120 Poles to 2 pines
N.W. 70 2 W O on a hill side
N 70 W 60 2 R O by a sink hole 620 Acres
N 35 W 40 2 W O
S 68 W 230 2 W O on a Spurr Rec.d Exam.d
N 60 W 120 2 W O by a meadow
S 32 W 20 ... two W O Willsons Corner thence ... Land
S 40 W 196 ... W O in a field S 25 E 140 ... on a hill side
N 85 E 166 ... on a hill side Willsons Corner
S 40 E 170 2 B O on a Ridge
N 85 E 100 4 pines in a hollow ... along the ... 219

An Addition to Col Stewarts Survey ...
beg at a W O ... next Corner to the Beg: of the former Survey
West 40 3 W O by a Branch
N 30 W 120 2 W O on a hill
West 160 Large pine on a Ridge
South 60 W O at the foot of a mountain ... along ...
to the Ending Corner of the former Survey

11th Octob.r 1754 the Whole amount to 400 Acres
when added

20

Page 70

23rd Feb'y 1754 - Surveyed for Ephraim Laud- - - on which he lives beg at — line — the foot of a hill nigh a n[orth] branch of Goose Creek thence ross the creek - adj. Willson's corner - 63 acres.

26th Feb'y 1754 - An adition [sic] to Col'o Stewards survey Martin Cove - beg. at a W.O. ye next corner to ye beg. of ye former survey - the whole amount to 400 acres when added.

****

N 55 E 100 by a branch down of same
S 55 E 78 Po. in a hollow 104 Acres
N 75 E 40 X y Back Cr. to on y S side & along the hill
to y Ending Corner of y former survey
4th Feb 1754 Rec Exd when added 1048

Surd for Thomas Ramsey on Burtons Run a branch of Catawba
at 2 W O corner to Burdens Entry thence

N 20 W 90 W O
N 35 E 78 W O
N 20 W 60 Double Ch.
N 35 E 86 W O on a shore
S 60 E 212 by a sink hole
East 76 2 Chts in Burdens line
Smith y same 297 Poles to y Beg

145 Acres
W Preston
Rec Exam

2d mar 1754

Surd for William Whiteside on a Branch of Glade Creek
beg at 2 W & B O corner to the Land on which he Lives

North 26 Poles to 2 W
N 30 E 58 thence
S 20 E 62 2 B O on a hill
S 40 W 80 2 pines on a ridge
S 40 E 40 4 W O
S 65 W 56 W O on a hill
N 20 W 56 3 W O by the Branch in his line
70 Poles to y Beg

54 Acres
16th July 1754
Wm Preston
Rec Exd

2d March 1754

Page 71

26 Feb'y 1754 - ____ Baird - addition - - - former survey - - - ye Back Ck. nigh on ye s[outh] side & along ye hill adj. Corner of former survey - 104 acres

2nd Mar. 1754 - Sur'd for Thomas Ramsay on Barrens Run at Boanin of Catawbo at 2 Cst O corner to Borden's entry thence... - 145 acres

Sur'd for William Whiteside on a branch of Glade Creek ... corner to the land on which he lives... - 54 acres

Clarrey [illegible]

on which he Lives Beg [illegible]

N 30 W 80 [illegible] of Branch [illegible] Popler [illegible]

S [illegible] W 200 Several Branches 3 W O on a hill [illegible] 10: [illegible]

South 100 3 P O on [illegible] end of a hill

+ [illegible] W 40, W O. 210 Acr

N 35 W 60, 2 B O. Rec.d Exam.

S 20 W 60 2 W O.

S 20 E 52 B O 2 W O Corner to Taylors Land & with his Line

N 70 E 28 Popler thence with that Line

S 54 E 60 4 W O Leaving the Same

N 35 E 36 [illegible] to the Beg

6th March 1754 363 poles [illegible]

RUN

Robt. Armstrong on McClure's [illegible] Branch of Buffelo Creek beg at 2 Black Walnuts by the branch

+ S 80 W 40 2 W O on a hill Rec.d Ex.d

S 40 W 120 W O B O in a hollow 70 Acres

S 20 W 100 4 W O

S 80 E 44 R O on a Ridge

N 40 E 42 W O on a hill [illegible] 103 Poles to the Beginning

16th March 1754

72

Page 72

6th March 1754 - Survey for Rob't Rennick ... on which he lives beg. - - - corner to Taylor's land & with his line... - 210 acres.
6th March 1754 - Rob't Armstrong on McClure's Run a branch of Buffelo Creek beg. At 2 black walnuts by ye branch - 70 acres.

ARTHUR McC

... for Arthur McC... ...ning the Land
...which he Lives ... a Branch of Buffeloe
Beg... at a ... on a hill Corner to the Pat Land thence
... 40 ...
N. W. 48 Poplar on a Ridge
S. W. 120 3 B.O.s
S 15 W 68 2 W.O.s on a Ridge
S 83 W 100 W.O.
S 66 poles 2 B.O.s on a hill
N 77 E 112 2 W.O.s by a Branch
S. E. 50 B.O. on a hill side
N 77 E 100 Lin & W.O. By a Branch
N 60 E 104 4 poplars
N 53 E 120 2 W.O.
N 35 E 76 2 B.O.s on a Ridge
S. W. 82 2 W.O.s on a hill
N 75 W 40 4 W.O.s
S 50 W 30 W.O.
N 25 W 120 3 W.O.s on a ridge & along the same to the Beg

Protract

11th March 1754 Some Mistake which Must be Rectifyd by going to the Place

73

Page 73

Surveyed for Arthur McClure running ye land on which he lives on a branch of Buffelos - Beg. At 2 B.O. on a hill corner to ye pat. Land thence. ..
"Some mistake which must be be [sic] rectify'd by going to the place." [written at the bottom of the entry]

7th Ap: [illegible] for [illegible]

on a hill side nigh the [illegible]

at a Sp: 176 WO

+ N,W, 60 Locust s on a hill

S 50 W 112 WO

S 40 W 80 WOs on a ridge

(Flat) S 50 E 46 pine thence 10 poles to ye Beg

70 Acres

Rec.d Ex:

Ap: 6th Surveyed for James Armstrong beg at a WO by a ?? of Branch of Gennings Branch in Clendinins Line thence

+ N 80 E 94 - 4 B O grubs in Thomas Bairds Line & with the same

N 54 W 118 WO

S 40 W 36 BO Corner to sd Armstrongs Land & with his Line

South - 94 X ye B' WO

S 25 W - 160 3 WOs

S 65 E 80 WOs

N 25 E - 48 BO

N 83 W 36 to Clendinins WO & with his Line

N,E, 66 BO on a hill

N 15 W 66 WO by the point of a hill thence Cross ye Run 56 poles ye Beg

100 Acres

Rec.d Ex.d

8th Ap: Survd for John Risk beg at a Large WO on a Spurr at the foot of a mountain thence

+ S,E, 70 BO in a Line of Birdens great Survey & with the same

S,W, 180 + a Small Bh. WO on a hill

N,W, 70 Sapling under ye Mountain & along the same

N,E, 180 to ye Beg

77 Acres

Rec.d Ex:

(17 July 1752 [illegible]) 74

Page 74

5th Ap'r 1754 - Survey'd for Thomas Baird [?] on a hill side night the land on which he now lives. - 10 acres

6th Ap. [1754] - Surveyed for James Armstrong - beg. At a W.O. by a small branch of Genings** Branch on Clendinin's line thence ... "grubs in Thomas Baird line & with the same".. Corner to s'd Armstrong's land & with his line - 100 acres

8th Ap: [1754] - Survey'd for John Risk - beg. At a large W.O. on a supurr [sic] at the foot of a mountain thence... adj "in a line of Borden's great survey & with the same." - 77 acres.

** Genings could be Jenings

****

... Survey ed for Wm Crisp... beg at a WO Corner to ... Mathew Edmeson's ...
... 15 W 36 WO ...
... 300 ... Barrens th:
... E 110 2 WO
S 65 E 80 near 2 WO in ye Naked Land
+ South 200 4 Bo Grubs at ye head of a Hollow
S 30 W 166 WO on a hill side
S 70 W 40 2 WO by ye Branch then to ye Beg 34 poles

(315 Acres)

6th Ap: 1754 Surveyed for Jn Rusk or Benj Kinsey on ye Water of Hays Creek a Branch of James River beg at 2 H^o at ye foot of a ~~hill~~ Mountain —
S 40 E 54 2 Ch^ts
S 10 W 60 3 H
+ S 10 E 36 WO
S 30 W 86 RO on a hill side
N 15 W 66 Large BO on a hill (Spring 20)
S 75 W 26 Ches^t
N 35 W 40 Ches^t under the Mountain & along the same 148 po to ye Beg

74 acres
Rec^d Ex^d

James Calhoune beg at 3 WO on a Ridge thence
S 75 E 72 x ye Spring BO
+ N 15 E 80 2 H by a path
S 40 W 146 3 H on a Ridge & along the same 160 poles to ye Beg
the above on ye Waters of Hays Creek a Branch of Js River

Rec^d Ex^d
64 Acres

5th April 1754
75

Page 75

Survey'd for Wm. Christal - beg. At 2 W.O. corner to the - - - of Mathew Emerson thence ... in the barrens ... 2W.O. in ye naked land - 315 acres.

8th Ap: 1754 - Surveyed for Jno. Risk or Benj'n Kinsey on ye waters of Hays Creek, a branch of James River - beg. At 2 H's at ye foot of a mountain - 76 acres.

8th April 1754 - James Calhoune - beg. At 3 W.O.s on a ridge thence - - - the above on ye waters of Hay's Creek a branch of Ja's River. - 64 acres.

****

Surveyed f[illegible] [illegible]
Calfpasture beg at [illegible]

+ S20 E 100 2 B O's in the Paten [illegible]
S 70 E 40 W O B O Corner to the Paten Line [illegible]
N34 E 90 W O in sd Line Recd Exd: 66 Acres
N50 W 100 2 W O at the foot of the hill & along ye [illegible]
11th april 1754 (58 po: to ye Beg

John Meek beg at 4 B O on a high Ridge by a path
S35 E 40 2 B O W O's Recd Exd:
+ N55 E 64, W O by a Spring
N20 E 60, B O on a hill side 100 Acres
N55 E 86, 2 W O on a Spurr of the hill Wm Beresford
N25 E 110, 3 B O on a Ridge
N85 W 60 W O on ye top of the Ridge & along the same
11th april 1754 1312 to ye Beg

Samuel Gay beg at 4 B O by Fletchers Spring
under the S Side the Mountain Recd Exd:
+ East 30 2 Gums
N10 E 130 3 W O's on the side of a hill 45 Acres
N E 40 W O
N65 W 54 W O on the North Side thence S30 W 60 po & South 110 along the same to the beg
11th April 1754

76

Page 76

11th April 1754 - Surveyed for Samuel Gay joining - - Calfpasture - beg. At - - at the foot - - adj. The Patent line. - 66 acres.

11th April 1754 - John Meek - beg. At 4 B.O.s on a high ridge by a path ... - 100 acres.

11th April 1754 - Samuel Gay - beg. At r B.O.s by Fletcher's Spring under the s[outh] side the Mountain.... - 45 acres.

****

[illegible] Daniel [illegible] WO in the [illegible] Land by the Road thence
[illegible] by a Draft
N 51 Large WO 100 Acres
N [illegible] W 100 Crossing some Small Branches of ye Calfpasture to 2 WO
+ Rec.d Ex.d
S 30 E 100 2 WO in Clemons Line & with the same 210 poles
23d April 1754

John William on a South Branch of Cowpasture beg at a Walnut & Asp by sd Branch under a hill S Side the rest
S 10 E 40 - 2 WO on a hillside
S 60 W 50 WO
+ West 60 WO Rec.d Ex.d 125 Acres
N [illegible] 40 - 2 WO by the Road
S 80 W 120 4 WO
N 55 W 40 + ye Branch Locust & two WO under the hill
N 13 E 184 thence along the same ~~[illegible]~~ to ye beg
23d April 1754

Hachlans Willson beg at 2 WO under a hill N Side ye River
+ S E 40 + ye River WO by ye hill thence up ye River
N 10 E 60 WO
N 80 E 180 WO Rec.d Ex.d 74 acres
N W 40 + ye River to WO on a high Shurt of the hill
S 40 W 176 & 80 poles along the same to the beginning
24th April 1754
77

Page 77

25th April 1754 - Samuel Campbell - beg. At a W.O. in the line of William Campbell's land by the road then...by a draft...crossing same & small branch of ye Calfpasture...adj. Clemon's line & with the same etc. - 100 acres.

25th April 1754 - John William on a south branch of Cowpasture - beg. At wal't & H. by ye s'd branch under a hill s[outh] side thereof...by the Road - 125 acres.

24th April 1754 - Hacklaw Willson - beg. At 2 W.O. under a hill n[orth] side ye River [James] - 72 acres.

****

Surveyed for [illegible]
Walk by the foot of [illegible] hill South [illegible]
S10W 70 - 3 Wo. thence to [illegible] up the River
+ N80E 70
N20E 124
N80E 40 — 130 Acres
S25E 50 + y River to a WO
N70E 40 WO by a Field — Rec.d Ex.d
N10E 80 WO on a hill side
N55W 66 2 WO at the foot of a hill thence
West 50 & thence along the hill S59W 68 to y Beg
62 poles
24th April 1754

Surveyed for Daniel Sharron a Small Branch of [illegible] beg at a [illegible] under the Side of a [illegible] Bank [illegible]
+ N40W 70 2 WO on a hill Rec.d Ex.d 18 Acres —
S50W 60 — WO in a Draft —
S40E 30 — pine & WO on y hill 73 poles [illegible] to y Beg
25th April 1754

Surveyed for Wm Price beg at a WO on the top of the
+ Bullpasture Mountain [illegible] opposite to Anglens
S70E 40 3 Chest.s
North 40 to a Chest.
N35E 70 2 WO — 50 Acres
N15E 40 [illegible] Rec.d Ex.d
N59W 80 2 pine on the Mountain [illegible] along [illegible] 173 poles
25th April 1754

78

Page 78

24th April 1754 - Surveyed for William Price - beg. wal't by the foot of steep hill south side... - 130 acres.

25th April 1754 - Surveyed for Daniel Shaw on a small branch of Cowpasture - beg. At a Sp.O. under the palide [palisade ?] of a steep bank..

25th April 1754 - Surveyed for Wm. Price - beg. At a W.O. on the top [?] of the Bullpasture Mountain oposited Anglens. - 50 acres.

****

McCANDLESS ON BRANCH

[illegible] Bullpasture [illegible]
[illegible] a draft of the branch [illegible] x of same
[illegible] E 60 Spanish O under a hill & along the same
[illegible] 90 Sp: O.
N 69 E 80 2 W O on a hill side
N 25 E 60 x of Branch to a W O
N. W. 48 Double W O
N 65 W 150 2 W O Rec: Ex:
N 25 W 40 – Chest
N 65 W 40 – Sp, O, & Chest on a hill & along the same 146 poles to beg.
26th April 1754

144 Acres
Land Wm. Preston
17th July 1754

Sur. for Charles Bodkin on a small Branch of Bull=
pasture begat at a W O Under a hill thence
N 55 E 34 + y e B, & a Maple Rec. Ex.
N 70 E 84 2 W O. on a hill side
N 40 W 68 W. O on a hill
S 70 W 60 2 W O by a Spring
S, W, – 110 2 Chest oaks in a draft – [illegible]
S, E, 86 – W O by the hill & along the same 80 Poles to beg.
26th April 1754

145 Acres

79

Page 79

26th April 1754 - _____ McCandless on a branch of Bullpasture [River ?] on a draft by the branch...& cross ye lane... - 144 acres.

26 April 1754 - Sur'd for Charles Bodkim on a small branch of Bullpasture beg. At a W.O. under a hill thence... - 115 acres.

****

Surveyed for ...
BULL PASTURE
Bullpasture beg...
to the Land of James Burnside
JAMES BURNSIDE
N60 E 56 3 poplars under the hill ...
N35 W 206 2 WO. in a draft
S40 W 74 2 WO. on a hill Rec. Ex: 125 –
S83 W 24 WO Corner to McCandless Land & with his Line
S25 W 60 – X y Branch S.P.O. under a hill & along the ...
192 Poles to y Beg
25th April 1754

Surveyed for Wm. Miller on a branch of Bullpasture
beg at 3 WO. at y foot of a hill on y West Side
S.W. 80 + y Branch to 2 pines
N.W. 80 WO on a hill
N25 W 90 2 WO's by the Draft 130 Acres
N50 W 62 Wal... at y foot of y hill
S70 W 72 WO
North – 48 WO in a hollow Rec. Ex.
N63 E 70 3 WO. at the foot of a hill ...
North 40 & thence 292 Poles along y hill to y beg
25th April 1754

Wm Preston D.S.M.

Wednesday y 10th July 1754 then, then, then, away, away, away went ...
to the inexpressible Pleasure of Wm Preston a former Devotee ...
who bowed at the Shrine of Venus —

80

Page 80

25th April 1754 - Surveyed for Samuel Forgison on Bullpasture beg. ... to the land of James Burnside...corner to McCandless land * with his line... - 125 acres.

25th April 1754 - Surveyed for Wm. Miller on a branch of Bullpasture beg. at 3 W.O. at ye foot of a hill on ye west side. - 130 acres.

[Note at the bottom of the page]

Wm. Preston V.D.M.

Wednesday ye 10th July 1754 then, then, then, away, away, away went

To the inexpressible pleasure of Wm. Preston a former devottee [sic] avoson [?] who bowed at the Shrine of Venus...

****

at McDonald side by Jackson

[illegible] side by Jacksons River

[illegible] Mast [illegible] under a hill

+ [illegible] down ye River to 3 WO^s

[illegible] 80 + ye River [illegible] to WO (100 Acres)

+ [illegible] 80 4 WO^s Rec.^d Ex.^d

[illegible] 40 + ye River to 3 WO on ye hill side [illegible]

North 50 thence 192 Poles to ye same by ye Beg — (Supposed to be 1500 or thereabout)

[illegible] 1754

Richd Collins on a small Branch of Jacksons River beg at 3 WO on ye East side of a small Meadow thence up ye same

[illegible] 40 2 WO by ye s^d Meadow

[illegible] 126 X ye Branch to 3 WO — Rec.^d Ex.^d Collins

+ N 35 W 110 X ye s^d Branch to a pine on a knobb [illegible] along ye hill [illegible] 160 Poles to ye Beg

[illegible] April 1754

John Bird on a Draft of Jacksons River beg at a pine on a hill on y^e [illegible] Side of [illegible] Branch thence Rec.^d Ex.^d

N 25 W 40 X y^e Branch 2 WO [illegible]

+ S 65 W 100 3 WO on a hill side — 48 [illegible] Bird

[illegible] South 50 + y^e Br. to a WO on y^e hill side [illegible] along y^e same to y^e Beg

30th April 1754

81

Page 81

29th Ap: 1754 - ________________ beg. At McDonald side by Jackson River - 100 acres.

- - April 1754 - Rich'd Collings on a small branch of Jacksons River beg. at 3 W.O. on ye east side of a small meadow thence up ye same... - 60 acres.

30th April 1754 - John Bird on a draft of Jacsons River beg. at a pine on a hill on ye s[outh] side ye branch thence. - 40 acres

****

BORELAND

James Boreland ...
Branch thence up ...
S 80 E 80 WO on a hill
+ S 25 W 74 + ye Branch to 2 WO
~~N 80 W 80~~
South 80 2 BO on a Ridge
N 80 W 80 3 Chestnuts on a hill by the Mountain & along the same 150 poles to ye Beg.

68 Acres

Recd. Exd.

Ap: 30th 1754

Surveyed for Alexander Macalvean on a Small Branch of Jacksons River beg at a WO by the Draft at the foot of a hill on ye South Side —
+ S. E 40 + ye Branch WO & pine
S 55 W 120 to Spanish Oak By a Branch
N 27 W 60 + ye Branch to 2 WOs on a hill & along the same N 27 70 & thence 76 poles to ye Beg

50 Acres

Recd. Exd.

2: May 1754

Phillip Houghey on a Branch of Jacksons River
+ beg at 2 WO. by ye Stoney Lick
S 15 E 20 WO
South 60 to an Ash
S 70 E 50 WO by a meadow
S 20 E 80 3 WOs
N 80 E 60 Maple
North 100 WO on a hill
N 40 W 60 WO on a hill side thence to ye Beginning

94 Acres

Recd. Exd.

82

~~...~~ Supposed

Page 82

Ap: 30th 1754 - James Boreland ... branch then up ye... 3 Ches't on a hill by the mountain & along the same. - 60 acres.

2nd May 1754 - Surveyed for Alexander Macalvean on a small branch of Jacksons River beg. at a W.O. by the Draft at the foot of a hill on ye south side. - 50 acres.

- - - Phillip Houghey on a branch of Jackson River beg. At 2 W.O. by ye Stoney Lick. - 94 acres.

****

JOSEPH ENGLAND

[illegible] for Joseph [illegible] both Sides Jackson's
[illegible] beg at 3 WO [illegible] ny N. Side thence up ye R
N 55 W 154 Rec'd Ex'd 85 Acres
N 10 W [illegible] crossing ye River to 2 Sug'r[illegible]
+ [illegible] ye R 2 WO on ye Bank (River 100)
S 20 E 40 [illegible] by a Gulley & Sout 41 Poles to ye Beg
[crossed out line]
3d May 1754
Surveyed for Edward McMullon on Both sides Jackson
River beg at a Bo & WO at ye foot of a hill
+ S 60 W 20 to an Ash by ye River Bank ye N side [illegible]
N 30 W 106 Rec'd Ex'd
N 10 E 20
N 70 E 100 up & + ye R 3 WO by ye hill (River 48)
S 65 E 160 3 Dogwoods 95 Acres
S 25 W 28 WO by ye Bank
N 65 W 70 Down & + ye River [illegible] on ye Bank
West 20 Sugr tree at a hill foot [illegible] ye same to ye Beg 102 Poles
4th May 1754
Surveyed for Jermiah Seely on ye Drip Stone a Branch
+ of Jacksons River ye S side beg at 3 WO at ye foot of a hill N side
S 40 W 40 + ye Branch to 2 Elms at ye foot of a hill (Branch
N 55 W 240 to a Large Pine at ye End of a hill [illegible] 100 Acres
N 40 E 40 + ye Branch to WO on ye side of a hill [crossed out]
S 86 E 70 & then 102 poles along the hill to ye Beg
5th May 1754 Rec'd Ex'd
83

Page 83

3rd May 1754 - Surveyed for Joseph England on south side Jackson's River beg. At 3 W.O. by ye bank on ye n[orth] side, thence up ye... - 85 acres.

4th May 1754 - Surveyed for Edward McMullon on both sides Jackson River - beg. At a B.O. & W.O. at ye foot of a hill... - 95 acres.

4th May 1754 - Surveyed for Jermiah Seely on ye Dry River, a branch of Jackson's River ye s[outh] side beg. At 3 W.O. at ye foot of a hill n[orth] side of branch - 100 acres.

Surveyed for Gabriel Jones on y[e] [illegible]
River beg at a [illegible] on y[e] West side of [illegible]
West 50 to a Sycamore on y[e] River's Bank
N 10 W 74 up y[e] River to [illegible] corner [illegible]
Rec. Ex:
N 80 E 80 BO on a hill & along the same 90 poles to y[e] beg
7th May 1754 Rec. Ex. 33 Acres

D[o] James Mountgomery on y[e] South side James River beg
at 3 WO in Thomas Hadleys Line & with the same
S 65 E 50 Double Walt. & [illegible] River thence up y[e] same
N 70 E 50
N 35 E 60 Rec. Ex. 80 Acres
N 10 W 80
North 42 to 2 WO on y[e] Bank thence
West 20 to a Chestnut Oak & pine on y[e] hill side & along y[e] same
7th May 1754 190 poles to the Beg

Do for James Mountgomery on y[e] North side James River
Beg at a BO on a hill side thence
S W 30 to a Mulberry by y[e] Bank thence down
S 40 E 110 54 Acres
East 44, 2 WO by y[e] River Rec. Ex.
N E 26 BO on a hill side ~~& along [illegible]~~ to y[e] beg
North 50 & along the hill 115 poles to y[e] Beg
7th May 1754

W[m] Preston
[illegible] 17th July 1754 Spring hill 84

Page 84

7th May 1754 - Surveyed for Gabriel Jones on ye New River - beg. At a Sp. O. On ye west side of the... - 33 acres.

7th May 1754 - S'd James Mountgomery [sic] on ye south side James River beg. At 3 W.O. in Thomas Hadley's line & with the same... - 80 acres

7th May 1754 - do for James Mountgomery [sic] on ye north side James River - beg. At a B.O. on a hill side thence. - 54 acres.

Note: "Wm. Preston - highs forrests [?] 17th July 1754 - Spring Hill"

DAVID GALLAWAY

[illegible] David Gallaway on a Branch of [illegible] Creek a Branch of Craigs Creek
beg at a W O on a hill nigh a Small Meadow thence
N 80 E 40 2 W Os by a Gully
S 70 W 44 Wall[illegible] 77 Acres
S 60 E 70 Span: O. in a hollow
S 10 W 100 Hiccory Rec.d Ex.d
S 80 W 40 Large W O in y Barrins & along y Same
N 30 W 84 & then South 100 Poles to y Beg
7 th May 1754

for John Martin on Lapsleys Run a Branch of Catabow beg at
W O on a hill side, nigh a Spring head thence
N 25 E 60 X y Run to B O on a hill
N 40 W 60 X D.o to B O 100 Acres
N 80 W 160 to 2 W Os (Run 60)
S 35 W 60 2 W Os by y Branch Rec.d Ex.d
South 40 X y Branch to a H on a hill & along y Same to y Beg 210 poles
8th May 1754

Surveyed for Samuel Lindsay on y N Side James River
Beg at a 2 W Os on a Ridge thence
South 34 po: a Mulberry by y River Bank & Down
East 60 Rec.d Ex.d
N 70 E 80 to a Spanish Oak on y Bank oposite to an Island
North 80 B O on a Ridge & along the same 47 Acres
154 Poles to the Beg
8th May 1754

85

Page 85

7th May 1754 - Surveyed for David Gallaway on a branch of —om Creek a branch of Craig's Creek - beg. At a W.O. on a hill nigh a small meadow thence... "large W.O. in ye barrens & along ye same..." - 77 acres.

8th May 1754 - For John Martin on Laps Legs Run a branch of Catabow - beg. At a W.O. on a hill side, nigh a spring head thence... - 100 acres.

8th May 1754 - Surveyed for Samuel Lindsay on ye n[orth] side James River - beg. At a W.O. on a ridge thence... - 47 acres.

****

Surveyed for [illegible] on [illegible]
Creek beg at a B O [illegible]
East 20 + ye Branch Dogwood
N 30 E 80 + ye Branch Several times to W O
West 60 + ye Branch 3 W O
N 40 W 80 + ye B: to W O on ye point of a hill
N 75 W 62 A B O Rec^d Ex^d
S 15 W 40 - + ye Creek to 2 W O on a hill ~~[illegible]~~
S 74 E 93 thence along ye hill to ye Beg 87 poles
11th May 1754

Surveyed for James Mc Callister on ye head Branch of Trees Creek beg at a poplar under a hill North Side the Branch thence
S 20 E 30 + ye Branch Spanish O
S W 52 W O 100 Acres
S 70 W 174 Chest^t & Maple on a hill side
S 35 W 60 3 Chest^s
S 50 W 70 an Ash by ye Creek Rec^d Ex^d
West 30 poplar on a hill side ~~[illegible]~~ Beg
N 86 E 184 thence 210 poles along the hill to ye Beg
11th May 1754

Surveyed for John Gillmore on Back Creek a Branch of Trees Creek beg at a W.O. Ash & R^d corner to his Patent Land th
N 15 W 80 B O Rec^d Ex^d 66 acres
S 75 W 100 B O on a hill side
S 10 E 120 2 Lins by the Bank ye Creek in the Patent Line of sd Land & with the same 120 poles to ye Beg
11th May 1754

86

Page 86

11th May 1754 - Surveyed for Willson McKenny on Back Creek - beg. At a B.O. ... - 90 acres.

11th May 1754 - Surveyed for James McCallistor on ye head branch of ye Ties Creek - beg. At a poplar under a hill north side of the branch thence... "poplar on a hill side & along ye lane to beg." - 100 acres.

11th may 1754 - Surveyed for John Gillmore on Back Creek a branch of Ties Creek beg. At a W.O., ash & H[ickory] corner to his patent land

****

— GLEON ? WATERS OF James River

[illegible] waters of James River beg at a [illegible] nigh Burdens Patent Line then along the Ridge
S 85 E 66 [illegible]
North [illegible] 130 W O
[illegible] 120 [illegible]
N 10 E 50 2 WO by a Spring
West 24 BO
S 50 W 80 Hiccory in the barrens nigh y Patent of Burdens Land & with y same 106 Poles to y Beg

110 Acres

Rec^d Ex^d

13th May 1754

CLYDES

Surveyed for David Clyde on the Waters of Roanoke Beginning at a WO & H nigh his Line on a hill thence
N 65 W 140 3 WO on a hill side
N 25 E 80 BO
N 55 E 160 H at the head of a hollow at or nigh his E^d Line & thence a Streaght Course to the Begining

113 Acres

20th Sepr 1754

Rec^d Ex^d

87

Page 87

13th May 1754 - - - - yle on ye waters of James River - beg. At a cht. & B.O.on a mountain [?] nigh Borden's Patent line then along that ridge... "hic[k]ory in the barrens nigh ye patent of Borden's land & with ye same 106 poles to ye beg." - 110 acres.

20th Sep. 1754 - Surveyed for David Clydes on the waters of Roanoke beginning at a W.O. & H[ickory] nigh his line on a hill thence... "at the head of a hollow at or nigh his s'd line & thence a streaght [sic] course to the beging [sic].
113 Acres

****

Surveyed for [illegible]
on the West side of [illegible] Creek, then [illegible] of Mudy Creek
North 200 Poles
N20W 34 Pine 251 Acres
West 140 2 pines
S20W 150 - 2 pines on a hill
S10E 74 2 P on a hill & along the same
190 Poles to the Beg: Recd Exd

+ 12th October 1754
James Bratton on Bratton Run beg at
a WO on y West side of sd Run nigh a corner to Dunlops
Land & with his Line
S43E 50 to a pine Recd: Exd:
+ S 55 W 200 cross several Branches 3 BO [illegible] of a Root
N W - 80 + y Run to a pine on a hill thence
N55E - 150 Poles & thence
a Streight Line to the Beg 90 Acres

21th Octobr 1754
Surveyed for James Gordon on a Branch of [illegible] Creek beg
+ at a Large Ch[illegible] oak on a hill West side the Branch
East 28 BO WO by y Bank thence down
S35E 34 Recd Exd: 54 Acres
S20E 20
S40E 120 + y B to a WO in Gamble's Line & [illegible] the same
S65 W 80 + y Branch to 2 Ch[illegible] on a hill & along the [illegible]

24th October 1754 18

Page 88

Surveyed for George Bigham beg. At - - - on the west side of Reedy Creek by a hill thence up the same. - 251 acres.

21st Octob'r 1754 - James Bratton on Bratton Run beg. at a W.O. on ye west side of s'd Run nigh a corner to Dunlops land & with his line... - 90 acres.

24th October 1754 - Surveyed for James Gordon on a branch of Ties Creek beg. at a large ch't oak on a hill west side the branch... adj. Gambles' line. - 54 acres

****

ROB'T WELLS TIES(?)

... Tees Creek beg

... adjoining the ...

... 60 ... on a Ridge

... 24 ... Oak on a Ridge

North 230 2 W O on a Ridge 126 Acres

N 65 E 60 2 W O on a hill side Rec.d Ex.d

S 80 E 60 + of B to 2 Sp O on ~~a hill~~ the S side of steep hill & along

Same to the beg --- 24th Oct.r 1754

Surveyed for John Gamble on a Branch of Tees Creek

beg at a Locust corner to Jacob Cunningham on the N side of Br.

& with the same

+ N 20 E 20 2 Sp O.

N 35 W 70 W O

North 54 - Ch Oak

West 40 2 Sp O on a Ridge

South 28 R O

S 65 W 168 + of B 2 H on a hill

S 25 E 54 H on a hill & along the same + of B to the Beg

This Survey is to be drop'd in Douglass's paying 116

24th Oct.r 1754 —

Wm. Gilmore on a Branch of Tees Creek beg at a W O & B O on a Ridg

N 60 W 42 B O on a Ridge

+ N 50 E 42 2 Ch.ts Rec.d Ex.d 67 Acres

East 96 2 Ch.ts

N 40 E 40 B O & Gum

N 60 E 80 - W O on a Ridge

S 35 E 48 - Ch.t

~~S 24~~ South 24 + Branch to a Linn on the hill side & along the same

25th October 1754 10/16 Promised

89

Page 89

25th Oct'r 1754 - Rob't Wells on Ties Creek - beg.... 126 acres.

24th Oct'r 1754 - Surveyed for John Gamble on a branch of Ties Creek, beg. At a loct's corner to Jacob Cuningham on ye west side of B'h & with ye same... [Note: This survey is to be dropped on Dougherdy's paying 1.4.6.]

25th October 1754 - Wm. Gilmore on a branch of Ties Creek beg. at a W.O. & B.O. on a ridge... - 67 acres.

****

Surveyed for ... James ______
fallen in Burdens ...
S 25 W 70 W.O. in ...
+ N 40 W 66 B.O. on a Ridge 54 Acres
N 25 W 74 2 W.O.s on a hill Rec.d Ex.d
N. E. 66 Ch.t Oak on a pine Ridge & along y ...

26th ap Octob.r 1754

Sur.d for Robert Young beginning at a Sp: O. & H on y West side
of a hill & runneth thence.
S 80 E 60 R.O. in Burdens Patent Line & with y same
S 25 W 72 to his corner H & Ch.t Oaks
S 40 W 40 B.O. —
S 10 E 80 — W.O.
+ S 60 W 30 3 W.O.s in s.d Youngs Pat. Line 154 Acres
N 50 W 18 W.O. B.O. nigh s.d Line
S 65 W 60 B.O.
S 23 W 32 B.O. in s.d Line & with y same
S 30 W 70 3 W.O.s
N 70 W 66 B.O. on a Ridge thence
N 30 E 160 ...
N 55 E 40 2 Ch.t Oaks on a Ridge thence along y same &c.

26 Oct.r 1754

90

Page 90

26th Octob'r 1754 - Surveyed for James - - - ...of a hill in Borden's line ... - 54 acres.

26 Oct'r 1754 - Sur'd for Robert Young beging [sic] at a Sp.O & H[ickory] on ye west side of a hill & runneth thence.... "B.O. in Borden's patent line & with ye same" - 154 acres.

Absolom Loony

... for Absolom ... beg at 2 Sp. O. at
... south side James River thence
N20 W46 Ash Hony Banks
S70 W180 Double Water
+ S10 E-20 3 BOs on a Ridge 240 Acres
S35 W 42 3 BOs
S20 E 100, 6 BOs
S75 E 130 WO
N65 E 84 3 WOs on a hill along y same Side Recd Exd

25th Octr 1754

for Priscilla Reise beg at a L by y foot of a hill on y south Side Catawbo Creek
S60 W100 X y Cr to a BO on a hill side
+ S30 E 50 BO
S7 W 100 BO, RO 134 Acres —
S35 E 60 3 WOs Recd Exd
S7 W 64 to y Cr up y same to an Ash
S83 E50 WO on a hill along y same Side
N13 E130 along the hill Side
30th Octr 1754

91

Page 91

28th Oct'r 1754 - Absolom Loony beg. at 2 Sp.O. at mouth of a branch on ye south side James River thence up ... - 240 acres.

30th Oct'r 1754 - For Priscilla Reese beg. At a H[ickory] by ye foot of a hill on ye south side Catawba Creek... - 134 acres.

Surveyed for ... Smith ...
Corner to his patent
Corner to his ...
N 60 W 80 B O & W O at head of a hollow
S 50 W 150 W O on a ledge ... a Branch
+ S 20 E 62 W O Rec.d Ex.d 254 Acres
S 10 W 20 3 R O by a Spring
S 30 E 44 Poplar Corner to Jos Snodgrass Land & near
S 25 E 120 to his 3 W O & with that Line this Line
S 50 E 44 Locust W O R O
N 80 E 20 to 2 W O corner to Sd Tobias Smiths Land
& with that Line to y Beg

30th Oct.r 1754
Henry Holston on Both sides of Craigs Creek Beg
at an Ash on y S side & C.k & Runs thence
S 70 E 68 2 Spruce
+ S 20 W 106 Sp.s O 338 Acres
S 70 W 58 2 W O
S 60 W 50 2 W O Rec.d Ex.d
S 30 W 90 2 Sp.s O
S 60 W 146 2 W O
N 50 W 90 + 76 ... 2 W O under a hill & along y same N 37 E ...
2d Nov.r 1754 & along y hill top ...

92

Page 92 - Surveyed for Tobias Smith beg. At a corner to his patent land & runeth thence... adj. Jos. Snodgrass lane and corner to s'd Tobias Smith... - 254 acres.

2nd Nov'4 1754 - Henry Holston on both side of Craigs Creek beg. At an Ash on ye s[outh] side s'd Ck & runs thence... 338 acres.

****

old survey thence

54 Acres

N. 40 W 120 3 gum & by a meadow Sold for £10 & I am to
N. 40 E 58 3 W.O. by the Branch make a free Patent
N. 50 E 120 Hiccory & the Branch 1 Augt. 1767 W.P.
East 22 BO in P. Line & with the same to the Beg.

1 Augt. 1767
~~10th Novr. 1754~~

Conrad Harchey on John's Ck. beg. at 2 W.O. his corner
to P. old survey Smith
S 15 E 00 & the Ck. 2 BO his corner
N 35 W 54 2 W.O. Rec.d Ex.d 73 Acres
N 45 W 00 3 W.O. above Harchey's old Place.
North 100 & the Ck. & old Ck. on the Bank thence the Ck. down

7th Novr. 1754

Surveyed for Wm. Preston on a small Branch of Lonie's
Mill Creek beg. at 2 B. J. on the End of a Ridge by the Branch
South 114 & the B. B. on the Ridge
S E 60 B.O. 125 Acres
N 50 E 140 2 B.O. on a hillside
North 54 4 W.O.
N 35 W 78 W.O. Corner to Mill Creek

first March 1755
Sold to, & made out for Mathew Hair

Page 93

4th Aug't 1754 - ______murtry [?] - ...old survey thence... - 54 acres
[Side note: "Sold for £10 & I am to make a free Patent - 7 Aug't 1767. W.P."

7th Nov'r 1754 - Conrad Harehey on John's Ck. Beg. At 2 Sp. O his corner... "above Harehey's old place..." - 73 acres.

First Month 1755 - Surveyed for Wm. Craster on a small branch of Lonies Mill Creek beg. At 2 B.O. under ye end of a ridge by a branch... "corner to Rob't Clark under s'd ridge..." - 125 acres

****

W. Bradshaw beg.

N 45 W 24 ash on ...

West 44 to ...

N 65 W 182 + ye Ch B O

N 55 W 36 2 W O by a Branch

S 50 W 174 W O

West 58 2 W O in a Bottom

South 50 + ye Ch to a hill ...

East 150 — & thence to ye Beg

1st Novr 1754

44
182
36
174
58
494 200

Surv^d for Wm Bradshaw on Stone Run a Branch of ... beg at 2 W O^s on ye N Side ye Run thence + ye same

South 54 B O W O
West 60 4 W O
North 30 ... tree
West 60 2 W O on a Ridge
North 80 + ye R B O at ye head of a hollow
6th Novr 1754

Rec^d. Ex^d.
54 Acres

East 60 along ... thence to ye Beg
(one course may be made)

Surveyed for John Patton on S^d Branch beg at a ... by a ...

N 30 W 48 B O on a hill
N 60 E 96 B O W O on a hill side
N 80 E 60 3 W O
S 85 E 164 2 W O
S 50 E 34 ... in Bradshaws line & with the same
South 60 + ye Branch 2 W O on a Ridge & along ...
6th Novr 1754 10/10 ... for ...

150 Acres
Exam^d Recorded

94

Page 94

1st Nov'r 1754 - Wm. Bradsh[aw]? Beg. ---- 200 acres.

6th Nov'r 1754 - Sur'd for Wm. Bradshaw on Stone Run a branch of Catabae - 54 acres

6th Nov'r 1754 - Surveyed for John Potts on s'd branch beg. At a W.O. by a — "...linn [lynn] in Bradshaw's line& with the same..." - 150 acres

Rec. Ex.^d

on a hill along the same 166 acres

1754

Ben.^n Davies on s^d Waters beg at 3 B^O at foot of a Mountain

North 52 2 W O

N 25 E 134 B O

N 65 W 48 B O by a spring — 114 Acres

N 25 E 13 + 4 p^l W O

S 72 E 134 W O on a hill

S 23 W 30 2 W O corner to Tho. Lees Survey & with his line

S 5 E 86 2 R O in a hollow thence along the same &c

7th Novr 1754

Daniel Loony on s^d Waters beg at a large Sp O & W O on the side of the Ck

N 10 W 100 + 8 ch Sp O.

S 80 W 74 — Protracted N 05 W 80

N 10 W 22 W O B — 204 Acres

S 80 W 44 W O

S 55 W 240 W O by a meadow

S 10 E 44 Pine on a hill & along the same

7th Novr 1754

Conrad Harchey on Johns Creek beg at W O his old sur. corner

N 60 E 140 4 W O — Rec.^d Ex.^d

S 30 E 120 + 6 ch 2 W O in a swamp

West 176 + 6 ch 3 W O in his old line & along the same beg

7th Novr 1754 — 68 Acres — 95

Page 95

6th Nov'r 1754 - ---- Bradshaw - continued from last entry.

7th Nov'r 1754 - Ben'n Davies on s'd water beg. At 3 Cts. At ye foot of a mountain ... "corner to the line survey & with his line..." - 114 acres

7th Nov'r 1754 - Davies Loony on s'd waters beg. At a large Sp. O. & W.O. on ye side of ck. - 204 acres.

8th Nov'r 1754 - Conrad Harehey on John's Creek beg. at a W.O. his old sur. corner. - 68 acres.

JOHN

N11 E 70
S77 W 34
S 80 W 120
South 68
S50 E 168
East 48
March 1753

150 Acres

Resurveyed for James Sandersdale ...

N 20 W 24
N 50 E 40
N 30 W 54
N 13 E 24
N 75 E 04
N 15 W 36
N 80 W 170
S 40 W 160

300 Acres

8th May 1753

96

Page 96

7th March 1755 - surveyed for John __________ - adj. his old Pat. Lands... - 150 acres.

5th May 1755 - Surveyed for James Lauderdale on a branch of ---- of Roanoke - beg. At 2 B.O. at ye foot of a hill on ye s[outh] side of ye ck... - 300 acres.

****

John Robinson Senr ... 8
John Robinson Junr ... 892
James Gorrell ... 610
Tobias Bright ... 695 ... 2477
George Pearis ... 176
Errick Bright ... 207
Elijah Isaac ... 370
Thos Hill ... 70 ... 854
3307
Col^o Patton ... 1000
Wm Pepper ... 500
Francis Cypher ... 400 ... 1900
5200
FRANCIS CYPHER

to JOSEPH HADLEY ABOVE SQUEEY

GREEN

122

At this point in the Note Book, the next surveyor turned the book upside down and backwards thus the page numbers change. These numbers were added by someone much later and they are not found in the original.

****

Page 121 - blank

Page 122

[What these names mean is anyone's guess:]

John Robinson, Sen'r	300
John Robinson, Jun'r	372
James Gorrell	620
Tobias Bright	635
George Pearis	176
Errick Bright	207
Elijah Isaac	370
Tho's Hill	70
Col'o Patton	1000
Wm. Pepper	500
Francis Cypher	400

Page 120 - 119 - Blank

Surveys by Wm. Preston on Roanoke

		Acres	
	Thomas Willson	041	H.
	Samuel Jackson	92	
	Wm. Boner	92	H.
	John McCurry	204	
	Wm. McCurry	80	
	John Robinson Senr.	70	H.
	Adam Lyday	104	
	Robert Bryson	65	H.
Catawbo --	Wm. Hutchison	20	H.
	James Davees	230	H.
	Joshua Hadley	95	H.
	James Bane	95	
	Adam Brineger	100	
	Thomas Brineger	66	
	John Highler	63	
H	Joseph Cummings		
H	Alexr. Ingram		
	Leonard Huff		
	John Mills — 4 Surveys		
	Martins Cave —		
H	Armstrong		
25 H.	Jno. McAdoo —		
	J. Neely 2		
	Daniel Morice — DANIEL MORICE		
	Patterson & Graham 2 — PATTERSON & GRAHAM		
	Hanley — HANLEY		
	Thomson — THOMSON		

117

Page 117

Surveyed by Wm. Preston on Roanoke:

Thomas Willson	41 A
Samuel Jackson	92
Wm. Boner	92 A
John McCurry	204
#5 Wm. McCary	80
John Robinson, Sen'r	70 A
Adam Lyday	104
Robert Bryson	65 A
Catawbo	
Wm. Hutchison	20 A
#10 James Davies	230 A
Joshua Hadley	95 A
James Bane	95
John Adam Briniger	100
Thomas Briniger	66
John Highler	63
#15 Joseph Cumings	
Alex'r Ingram	
Leonard Huff	
John Mills - 4 surveys	
Martins Cave	
Ann Armstrong	
Jno. Macadoo	
Jno. Neely - 2	
Daniel Morice	
Patterson & Graham	
______ Hanley	
________ Thomson	

****

Wm Baird
Jo McCormick
Wm Armstrong
John Thomas
Irwin Patterson 5
Alex Ingram
Ep: Vause
Jo Boyle
Jn Donnily
Wm Snodgrass -- 10
James Lauderdal
James Lauderdale
Charles Milligan
John Patton
Wm Ralston -- 15
Hugh Carothers
James Elliot
James Patton
Luke McEhenry
Jn Pritchard --- 20
James Davies
John Marshall
Ditto
Thos Ramsay
Isaac Lindsay 25
Geo: Hollis
Jas Hollis
Neal McNeal
Wm Carvin ---
Thos Bringer 30

Jas Patton 3
Harger - 1
Alex Walker 1
Jn Smith --- 1
B Merrit 1 — 37
Mills of Miller 1 — 38

Miles Ct. near NIGH
mill place MILL PLACE
Little bottom LITTLE BOTTOM
Wolf Creek WOLF CREEK

4/21

WM CARVIN
THOS. BRINIGER

118

Page 118

Wm. Baird		
Jos. McCormick		
Wm. Armstrong		
John Thomas		
Erwin Patterson -		5
Alex'r Ingram		
Ep. Vause		
Jno. Boyle		
Jno. Donnily		
Wm. Snodgrass		10
James Lauderdal [sic]		
James Lauderdale		
Charles Milligan		
John Patton		
Wm. Ralston		15
Hugh Carothers		
James Elliot		
James Patton		
Luke McTheny		
Smitchard		20
James Davies		
John Marshall		
Jas. ditto [probably Jas. Marshall]		
Thos. Ramsay		
Josiah Ramsay		25
Geo. Hollis		
Jas. Hollis		
Neal McNeal		
Wm. Carvin		
Thos. Briniger		30
Jas. Patton	3	
Hargis	1	
Alex. Walker	1	
Jno. Smith	1	
B. Sterrit	1	37
Mills & Miller		38

Mills Ct. Nigh
Mill Place
Little Bottom
Wolf Creek

****

James Brooks grave yard in Pattons field

James Brooks [illegible] grave yard in Pattons field

East by poles
South by Ditto
West 6½
North 6½ } ¼ of an Acre

John Donely Entered 100 a[cres] of ye Big Spring by his House on ye N. E. Side of his Land

Jno. Mills 400 ac — To enter for Jno. Mills 400 acres between [illegible] Dutch Coopers & [illegible]

Jno. Martin — To Enter for Jno. Martin [illegible] on Pattersons Creek [illegible] the White Walnut Pattons [illegible]

To Enter for Wm. David Walker [illegible] Land on ye head Waters of [illegible]

John Lowry — To Enter for John Lowry 200 acres on ye [illegible] Lewis Gillespie Land

[illegible] by Robt. Mongomery

115

Page 115

James Burks grave yard in Patterson's field - 1/4 acre

John Donely entered 100 at ye ____d Big Spring by his house on ye S.E. side of his land.

[The following was upside down on the page coming from front to back.]

Enter for Francis Lindsay ....

To enter for John Lowry - 300 acres on ye - - - Denis Getty's land.

To enter for Wm. Baird 400 acres ..... taken from the hands land on ye head waters of Roanoke.

To enter for Jno. Martin 200 acres between Hays' house on Patterson's css'l [?] and ... the White Walnut Bottom ....

To enter for Jno Mills 400 acres between Jas. [?] Lauderdale and Dutch Coopers & 400 acres between Jas. [?] Lauderdale and ....

Sur. John Robinson Jr: Lying on both sides Goose
Creek Beg: at a W.O. [illegible] N10 W60
to 2 W O N30 W 144 to a W O nigh his house
N8 E 226 to 2 W O:
N11 W60 to 3 W O: by a Branch th:
S79 E 270 Poles Crossing y: River to 1 B & W O to y: River both [illegible]
the Pat: Line to y: Beg:

Sur for James Gorrell on both sides Goose Cree[k]
Beg at a [illegible] & W O nigh y: Mountain on the S side of sd
Creek [illegible] being corner to Jn: Robinsons Land & with
his Line
N79 W 270 Crossing y: River to y: same 210 to 3 White O: by a branch his corner
N11 W 192 1 W O Sap:
N10 E 152 1 W O by a Branch
S72 E 254 1 W O Sap: to y: River 170 thence to y: Beg:

Sur for Tobias Bright Beg at 1 W.O. Sap: being Gorrells
Corner And with the same N72 W 254 to his W O by a Branch
S10 E 96 to 2 W O:
N60 E 300 to 3 B O: on a hill
S65 E 240 to y: mountain 70 to y [illegible]
5th of Dec: 17[illegible]

116

Page 116

Sur'd John Robinson, Ju'r lying on both sides Goose Creek - beg. At a W.O. corner to John Robinson, S;'r ... nigh his house... running along the Pat. Lines to ye beg.

Sur'd for James Gorrell on both sides Goose Creek - beg. at a pine & W.O. nigh ye mountain on the s[outh] side of s'd creek thence being corner to Jno Robinson's line & with his line

26th Dec'r 175? - Sur'd for Tobias Bright - beg. At 1 W.O. Leaving Gorrell's corner and with the same....

****

27th December 1752
Surveyed for Mr. George Pearis a Tract of Land on Both sides Goose Creek, Beg: at 3 B O: on ye S Side of the Creek being a Corner of Tobias Brights Land ~~[illegible]~~ & with the Pat Line
N 60 E 140 to 2 W.O. Sapp. thence
S 47 E 100 to ye mountain
2d Beg at 2 red O Sap 67 yds from ye Corner
(to ye River 40)

Surveyed for Enoch Bright a Tract of Land on both Sides of Goose Creek Beg: at 2 W.O. Sapp. Corner to the Land of George Pearis & with ye Pat Line
N 60 E 72 to 2 W O. on a Steep hill
S 45 E 32 to a Hicory by a Branch crossing ye Same
N 60 E 58 to 3 W O: Saps:
S 40 E to ye River 40 poles thence to ye Pat Line on ye N Side

---

Surv'd for Elijah Isaack on both sides Goose Creek Beg at 3 W.O. Sap: being Corner to Enoch Brights Land
N 60 E 162 to a W.O.
S 40 E to ye River from thence to ye mountain 130 poles

113

Page 113

27th December 1852 - Surveyed for Mr. George Pearis a tract of land on both sides Goose Creek, Beg. At 3 B.O. on ye s[outh] side of the creek being a corner of Tobias Bright's land & with the pat. Line.

Surveyed for Errick Bright a tract of land on both sides of Goose Creek - beg. at 2 W.O. sap'n corner to the land of George Pearis & with ye Pat. Line.

Surv'd for Elijah Isaach on both sides Goose Creek - beg. at 3 W.O. sap. being corner to Enoch Bright's land...

****

27th Decr. 1752
Thomas Hill on Both sides Goose Creek Beg at a W.O.
Corner to Elijah Isaac's Land thence with ye Pat Line
N 60 E 64 W.O.
N 45 E 28 to a W.O. S 30 E (130 to ye River 25 poles)

29th Decr. 1752
Sd. Col. James Patton on both sides of Goose Creek Beg. at
a W.O. sap: at Thomas Hills Corner & with the Pat: Line then
N 45 E 400 to 2 B.O. on a Rock hill (to a run 280) th:
S 50 E 180 to ye Creek & the same Course to ye mountain.

Wm. Pepper 1 Tract on Goose Creek Beg. at 2 B.O. in
Col. Patton's Corner thence with ye Pat: Line
N 45 E 294 to a Black Oak on a Hillside
S 52 E 40 to Elijah's Branch from thence 50 po: to ye River

Francis Cyphers Beg at a W.O. in Wm. Peppers corner
N 45 E 238 to a W.O. on a high hill
S 45 E 200 to a W.O. on a mountain (to ye River

114

Page 114

27th Dec'r 1752 - Thomas Hill on both sides Goose Creek - beg. at a W.O. corner to Elijah Isaac's land thence with ye pat. Line.

27th Dec'r 1752 - S'd Col'o James Patton on both sides of Goose Creek - beg. At a W.O. sap. At Thomas Hill's corner & with the Pat. Line thence...

Wm. Pepper 1 tract on Goose Creek - beg. at 2 B.O. in Col'o Patton's corner thence with ye pat. Line...

Francis Cyphers - beg. at a B.O. in Wm. Pepper's corner....

****

Decr. 30th. 1752 John Robinson on Both Sides of Goose Creek Beg: at a W O on ye S side of ye Creek N75 W 280 Crossing the River to 2 W Os. N10 W 100 to a W O N75 E to ye River 40 Crossing a Branch to ye Mouth ...

Ben Ogle on Both sides of Goose Creek beg: at a W O ... to Thomas Rice N45 E 72 ... S37 E 100 ... to ye River, from thence ... ye Open ...

118

Page 111

Dec'r 30th 1752 - John Robinson on both sides of Goose Creek - beg. At a W.O. on ye s[outh] side Creek.... crossing a branch of ye mountain.

Ben Ogle on both side of Goose Creek by a W.O. corner to Thomas Hill....

FARRIS CREEK

January 1753 Toms Creek Survey

Beg at 2 WO: at a Spring N 69 W 434 to a W O in the Pat Line
in a course S 07 W 32 to 2 Hicory Grubs W. the sd Patt line
N 37 E 192 B O, W O & H, Et. 60 to a Stake N 98 2 pines N 69 E 60 3 W O
N 40 E 144 [illegible] N 77 E 124 [illegible] 54 [illegible] Cabin) 160 to a field. [illegible]
N 69 W 140 to a [illegible]
180 to a H by a spring. 180 to a B O [illegible] Branch of sd Willow meadow
126 to Toms Creek

Wm Leperd S 67 W 320 to 2 B O & 1 W O [illegible] S 2 32 E 242 3 W O [illegible]
by the Lick Run S 47 E 526 1 W O in sd Pat line from thence to sd
corner N 55 E 38 to near a blazed W O.
from the Lick Run corner S 63 E 346 to a W.O. B.O. H. corner to the
Land of Casper Barrier
from thence be

Casper Barrier, Beg at 3 W O [illegible] by a Draft in [illegible] Line
S 35 E 160 to 2 W O [illegible] a H: (to a [illegible] 60) [illegible] W 140 3 W O [illegible] by a Draft
S 10 E 100 to a W O (to a Run 50) ~~[illegible]~~
~~Line thence N 17 W [illegible]~~
E 220 to 2 W O & a Hicory [illegible] South 134 W O B O & H [illegible] line [illegible]
sd same N 65 E 345 to sd Lick corner
Jn. Draper Beg: 2 B O 2 W O [illegible] line
S 67 W 470

Jacob Harman Beg at 2 B O, W O, [illegible] N 75 W 320 [illegible]
to a Run 200

112

Page 112

January 1753 - Tom's Creek survey - beg. at 2 W.O. at spring.... in the pat. Line ,,, branch of Willow Meadow/ 126 to Tom Creek

Wm. Seperd [Shepherd ?] ... by the Lick Run.... in ye pat. Line from thence to ye corner... corner to this land of Casper Barrier... from thence beg.

Casper Barrier - beg. By a draft in Echerd's line .

Jacob Harman - beg. At 2 B.O. - ...

S67 W 470 / No 1 BO 100 poles
2 BO. 100
3 Lin W. 100 to a Run 60
4 WO. 100 to a Run 30
5 2 BO. 1 WO H. 70 to Harmans Corner

Prices Land Beg: at 2 BO. 1 WO 1 H: by a path in Harmans Corner
S. 18 W 303 to a pine in the Barrens / N1 WO saps by a Cabin,
N2 to a Blazed burnt tree [illegible] the Barrens No 3 to a pine the [illegible]
South 88 to a WO. by a field, East 40 to 3 Hiccory saps
S - - 68 to 4 WO saps in the Pat Line & with the same
West 28 to a Large Spreading Pine in a Glade
Larsons Line Beg: 2 BO. 1 WO 1 H by a path
S67 W 710 poles to a Double WO & 2 WO saps in a Hollow
No 1 to Near a Large WO 100 poles
2 to 2 WO. 100 (to a Run 30)
3 to 3 pines — 100
4 3 W & a pine by ye Dams 100 —
5 to a Lowsp in the Barrens
6 to 6 WO. saps in a Hollow
7 to the Pat Line 110 — from thence — 710

~~N12 E 160 to 2 WO & H saplins by a Draft & from the S.~~
Corner Double WO & 4 & S 12 W 166 poles to [illegible] between 2 Large
WO & 2 [illegible] saps on the [illegible] of the Waggon Road

1753

109

Page 109

Price's land - beg. At 2 B.O., W.O., 1 H[ickory] by a path in Harman's corner ... a pine in the barrens... by a cabin... to a blased burnt tree... waggon road.

Page 108 - blank

Jacob Lingel Beg at 2 BO & 1 WO Saplins Corner to the Land of Casper Barrier & with his Line

S 22 E 80 to 3 WO 1 BO Saps by a Glade thence

S 40 W 220 to two H. Saps in a Hollow

S 12 E 90 to a H: & 2 WO Saps on a Barren Ridge

S 32 W 124 to between a H & WO on a Ridge (to ye Run 118)

N 36 W 200 to between 3 WO by a path corner to Col Patton

Thence to ye Beg 12th Jan^y

Col Patton Beg at 3 WO by a path corner to Lingell

S 15 W 315 to a BO tree & WO Sap: in ye Barrens

S 12 E 74 to near a WO & pine by the Great Road in the Pat Line & with the same

West 78 to three Pines in a Cluster

Hugh Mills on the Welshmans Run beginning at 2 BO 1 WO corner to his Pat Land thence

West 62 3 BO Crossing the Ck

N 35 W 46 2 BO

N 55 E 40 Cross the Branch to 2 BO on a high hill thence

19th Sep^t 1753 82 Poles along ye same to ye Beg

18. Acres

110

Page 110

12th Jan'y 1753[?] - Jacob Lingel - beg. At 2 B.O. & a W.O. saplin corner to land of Casper Barrier & with his line... by a glade thence... on a barren ridge...by a path corner to Col. Patton thence to ye beg.

Col. Patton - beg. At 3 W.O. by a path corner to Lingell...W.O. & pine by the Great Road in the Pat. Line & with the same...

Hugh Mills on the Welshman's Run beginning at 2 B.O. & W.O. corner to his pat. Line thence... - 18 acres.

****

Begat a Chesnut & 130 Peich Survey on a Ridge PEICH SURVEY

N 65 E 332 to a Hicory by a Branch

S 25 E 40 R.O, W.O, H,

N 65 E 544 to R.O. on a Mountain (Lynam Run 192) (meets 456)

S 53 E 40 to a tall B.O,

N 49 E 120 W.O in a Hollow,

S 68 E 64 2 W.O Grubs

S 41 W 96 to a forked Grub

S 11 W 34 B.O H,

N 82 E 64 to a Grub on the Top of a narrow Ridge

East, 44 to a bending W.O in a Hollow

S 37 W 04 2 W.O by a brook

S 07 E 40. N 73 E 70 to a parcel of Grubs -- to protract

S 27 E 80 B.O. H.

S 57 W 180 to an ash

S 69 W 200 between 2 W.O & a Chesnut on a hill

N 22 W 10 forked Ches & B.O

S 69 W 14 to between 2 Branches & Double W.O

[illegible] of Br of Sdina & 370 to a Double W.O,

[illegible] B.O

[illegible] by a [illegible]

Page 105

Beg. At a chestnut & B.O. on a spur of Peich survey... on a spur of Lynam Run... [the rest of the page is surveyor's calls.]

****

Mc DUNNALS

Joseph McDonnal's Dividing Line from Geo: Robinson
begining at [illegible] 2 Sp O & a H in Renfroes Line

S 25 W 200 Double Ch[illegible] WO's   18th Sepr. 1753
N 62 W 20 - Sp O
S 25 W 86 2 WO's
N 10 E 60 H by a meadow
N 55 W 46 Cross the meadow to a H[illegible]

Joseph Robinson part of George Robinson[illegible]
beg at a WO in his Line by Tinkers Creek thence
N 35 W 40 X the Creek Bank
N 60 E 46 3 RO's
South 62 X Creek to 2 WO's in sd Line [illegible]
9 Acres

107

Page 107

Joseph McDonnals dividing line betw. Geo. Robinson beginning at... in Rentfrow line... by a meadow.

Joseph Robinson part of George Robinson pat. Beg. at a W.O. in his line by Tinker Creek thence. - 9 acres.

Beg. at a WO by a meadow on Little Pine River

N65½W 172 to 2 WOs

S70W 66 to a large WO tree & BO to Protract from by it

S80W 150 to a Cluster of S by a meadow

N22W 32 to a Parcel of S

S52W 100 to a BO on a Ridge

S22E 22 BO H

S52W 92 4 WOs

S22E 30 3 WOs by a Branch

S68W 366 BO WO to WO 100 Bending WO 100 BO on ridge 100

S79W 140 WBO

S10E 20 to 3 Saps WO H

S79W 112 BO H (bottoms 40 to Branch 16)

N18W 12 2 WO

S72W 80 WO BO H

N70W 44 lau BO

S71W 108 Double WOs

S82W 160 between 2 Ridges

N35E 242 walnut

N73E 60 between 2 WOs

S57E 120 large WO

N75E 132 2 BO

N5E 00 to a Stake

W 40 WO

106

Page 106

Beg. At a W.O. by a meadow and the Pine Run ... [the rest of the page is just calls for surveyor's markings]

N 20 E 260 BO on a Spurr
N 25 W 192 BO WO
N 65 E 190 BO W Chesnut
N 25 W 20 L. B.O. on a Spur
N 65 E 194 H Grubs near 2 BO
S 25 E 20 WOs in a Volly
N 65 E 58 Parcel of Grubs near BO
N 24 W 40 Larg BOWO on a Spurr Beg: –

North 13 W 370 to between 2 Hicory & BO on a Ridge
to the Great Road Crossing Pine Run (226)

B at a B.O. on a hill
N 60 E 420 to a BO on a Ridge ((to big pine Run 186 Babcsk Run 353)) 353
S 60 E 182 2 BOWO on a Strong Ridge to Lynams Road 70
N 80 E 480 to ye above 2 Hicory & BO on a Ridge
(to Little Pine Run 390)

103

Page 103

[mostly surveyor's calls] "...between 2 Hic[k]ory & B.O. on a ridge to the Great Road crossing Pine Run..."

The notes of Drapers Survey

Beg. at 3 WO. on the West side of the Ridge that Divides Roanoke & new river Waters Thence

N 10 Dg. E 180 H WO Chestnut
N 80 W - 180 WO. BO. H near 2 WO.
N 10 E - 70 BO between RO & WO east side of Branch up.
N 60 E - 140 Between 2 BO 3 Ch:
N 17 W 88 2 WO. in a narrow Valley
S 70 W 164 2 Ch:
N 35 W 100 H WO near ye head of a spring
S 70 W 30 between 2 W
N ---- 120 2 WO
E ---- 70 2 H near a Cluster of WO
N 14 E - 40 WO & 2 WO
N 60 E - 78 near a BO & WO Bald hill.
N 15 W - 222 BO WO foot of a Pine Hill
S 60 W 140 3 pines side of a piny hill
S ---- 26 3 WO near 2 BO. head hollow
S 54 W - 90 BO between two H on ye side Tom's
N 60 W - 40 Cross in Toms Creek to 2 Dogwoods
S 30 W 54 2 BO. WO 102
S 77 W - 104 Stake on the side of a Hill
S 40 W 144 [illegible]
[illegible] W 6[illegible]

Page 102

The notes of Draper's Survey - beg. At 3 W.O. on the west side of the ridge that Divides Roanoke & New River waters thence... "crossing Toms Creek..."

Page 101 - blank

Due South 92 to a Stake near a Large WO Small BO
West - - - - 60 BO WO H on ye point of a ridge
S 37 W - - 166 2 H Grubs near 2 BO on a ridge
S 75 W - 140 Stake near a Large Spreading WO
S - - - - - 46 2 Bucky under a Rock
S 35 W - - 50 *
S 62 W 236 2 WO
N 31 W - - 20 to a Stake in ye Barrens
S 59 W 60 to a pine on a Ridge
S 9 E 34 H 2 WO
S 81 W 100 WO Double WO by a Gully
S 10 W 22 BO 2 pines
N 80 W 136
N 86½ W 50
S 62 E - - 216 2 WO H on ye E side of a Ridge
S 1½ E 300 to a Stake between 2 WO & a Locust
S 60 E - 120 WO near a BO
N 47 E 60 Large WO
E - - - 80 3 WO
... 80 3 WO near a pine Grove

99

Page 99

Due south 92 to a stake near a large W.O. small B.O.
[surveyor's calls]

****

S19 E 160 2 sorrel & WO saplins 2 pines by a Gully
S62 E 30 f.
N55 E 62 forked pine head of a Bottom
N3 E 88 3 pines by a Brook — 140 / 78 / 62
N59 E 62 W
S31 E 20
N59 E 114 2 LWO
E ..... 78 RO 2 WO
N 57 ... 59 Spreading pine
E ..... 94 2 pines on ye side of a naked tree
S ..... 24 3 pines in a Cluster
East .. 140 Small pine in a Glade
S40 E .. 94 4 WO & RO Grubs by a meadow
N75 E ... 70 WO 3 WO Grubs near a Bending W
S16 E .. 20 BO tree piny ridge
N86 E ... 226 3 WO near a Spring
N40 E --- 146 - 2 WO trees
S 65/69 E 85 to a Spreading pine
S72 E --- 108 - to a pine
N55 E ... 120 to a Stake in the Barrens by WO
N11 E .. 300
N44 W .. 140

100

Page 100 [primarily surveyor's calls]

3d May 1758 Dividing
Edward McDonnald Part of a tract of 140 Acres Deeded
by Col Patton beg at 2 WO Hs corner to his old Pat Land by with
the same crossing the Branch 60 poles to a BOWO trees
on a hill thence
East ---- to a Hickary in a Hollow th:
N 37 E 36 2 WO in sd Line (which line continues further)
N 33 W 60 Cross the Branch to 4 Hs in a Line of sd 140 Acres
and with the same (which line begin at a WO in a glade)
S 37 W 20 3 WOs by the road thence with one short course
to the Beginning the uper part to Joseph McDonnald

100 Acres

98

JAMES NEELY

Page 98

3rd May 1753 - Edward McDonnald dividing part of a tract of 140 acres deeded by Col. Patton beg. At 2 W.O. & H. Corner to his old pat. Land & with the same crossing the branch 60 poles to a B.O. W.O. trees on a hill thence... "to the beginning the uper [sic] part to Joseph McDonnald.

14th April 1755 - James Neely ... on a high bank... his corner & with his line & a..." - 100 acres

****

Wm Thos & Jno Robinsons Land notes
Beg a 2 popolar & an ash near a fall
S 71 E 86 ash sug tree in a Spring
N 16 E 234 B O
N 38 E 56 H WO on a B:
N 43 W 32 WO H
N 04 W 174 WO
N 15 E 38 H
N 41 E 62 B O — 41 —
S 02 W 114
[illegible] W 350
[illegible]

by Mr Poage fell short 150 acres

uper Place

Beg a 2 sycomores on ye Creek
S 0 W 550
N 02 E - 114
N 41 E - 78 B O
N 21 E - 166 B O WO
N 54 W 78 2 WO
N 7 E - 160 WO
N 34 W 76 WO & BO
[illegible] 60 WO
[illegible] 60 —

Page 97

Wm. Tho's & Jno. Robinson's land notes - beg. At 2poplar & an ash near a fall... "by Mr. Poage fell short 150 acres..."…. "uper [sic] place"

Heritage Books by James L. Douthat

1832 Creek Census

Alabama Soldiers in the Cherokee War

Augusta County, Virginia Survey Book of James Patton and William Preston, 1752–1755

Burke County, Georgia Records, 1758–1869

Cherokee Reservoir Grave Removals by T.V.A.

Chickamauga Reservoir Cemeteries

Early Wythe County, Virginia Settlers

Early Settlers of Montgomery County, Virginia: 1810–1850 Virginia Census

Fort Loudon Reservoir Cemeteries

Grainger County, Tennessee Various Records, 1796–1848

Hiwassee Reservoir Cemeteries

Jefferson County, Tennessee Will Book 1, 1792–1810

Jefferson County, Tennessee Will Book 2, 1811–1833

Kentucky Lake Reservoir Cemeteries, Volumes 1–3

Montgomery County, Virginia Will Book I: 1786–1809

Sequatchie Families

Sequatchie Valley Bible Records

Watauga Reservoir Cemeteries

Williamson County, Tennessee Tax Listings 1800–1801, 1805